Zum umstehenden Farbbild: Rom. Santa Maria della Vittoria. Hochaltar.
Die Verzückung der hl. Theresia von Avila. 1646, von Gian Lorenzo Bernini.
Colour picture overleaf: Rome. Santa Maria della Vittoria. High Altar.
The ecstasy of St. Theresa of Avila. 1646, by Gian Lorenzo Bernini.

EUROPEAN SCULPTURE

BAROQUE
SCULPTURE

With an Introduction by

WERNER HAGER

Edited by

HARALD BUSCH AND BERND LOHSE

With Commentaries on the Illustrations by

EVA-MARIA WAGNER

LONDON
B. T. BATSFORD LTD

TRANSLATED BY PETER GORGE

FIRST PUBLISHED, 1965

ALL RIGHTS RESERVED

© UMSCHAU VERLAG · FRANKFURT AM MAIN 1964

PRINTED AND BOUND IN GERMANY
BY BRÖNNERS DRUCKEREI BREIDENSTEIN KG · FRANKFURT AM MAIN

FOR THE PUBLISHERS, B. T. BATSFORD LTD.
4 FITZHARDINGE STREET, PORTMAN SQUARE, LONDON, W. 1

A vast legacy of sculpture, in metal, stone, wood, stucco, terracotta and other materials, survives (despite the immense damage wrought by war, ignorance and decay) from the period of European history that falls between the middle of the sixteenth and the end of the eighteenth century.

The term 'Baroque sculpture' embraces the output of the entire Continent over 200 years, although it might seem to apply more accurately only to the art of the seventeenth century. A more precise classification would place the Baroque proper between the Mannerism of the Late Renaissance and the Late Baroque, which is generally called — not altogether accurately — the Rococo. In applying the concept Baroque to the entire epoch, emphasis is, however, given to the unifying aspect that transcends all distinctions and metamorphoses, a unity that reflects the whole character of an age which has its roots in the Renaissance and the Reformation and ends with the French Revolution. Its manifestation through the arts is so vigorous that it has come to be generally described on the Continent as the Baroque Age.

Baroque sculpture evolved from its beginnings in the Italian Renaissance in a continuous development, though twice profoundly affected by changes in the concept of the world. The first crisis came around 1530 when the Renaissance passed into Mannerism, the second towards 1590, at the turning point from Mannerism to the Baroque. This style, however, subject to inevitable modifications, passed without further breaks into its late phase.

The art of the Renaissance marks a profound revolution. Whereas medieval man had seen the world as a mirror that reflected the working of the Divine, the whole of nature now appeared as the result of cause and effect. Man achieved a new self-awareness, and the whole quality of life changed towards greater freedom and diversity. Thought at the beginning of Modern Times was dominated by Greek philosophy, though man's guiding image — the concept of the unity of the cosmos, full of purpose and meaning — was still rooted in the Christian teaching of a created world moving towards redemption; it was an image only the enlightenment of the eighteenth century was to doubt and finally to reject. Sculpture was therefore faced with the task of evolving further the traditional religious imagery and at the same time of reflecting the secular life of man. The necessary proximity to nature was gained by the study of anatomy and psychology, while the ideal of the harmonious beauty of the human form, the study of proportion, originated in the school of Classical sculpture.

The Age of Mannerism

Since the advance of knowledge in the Renaissance did, as yet, not undermine the religious foundations of the age, a renewal of faith automatically followed the renewal of thinking. But the reformation of the body of the Church failed: the Christian world was split into a plurality of creeds. Purified and strengthened in faith, the Catholic Church soon turned against the secularism of the Renaissance, and at the same time took up the struggle against Protestantism. Persecution and civil war became the mark of the age; on both sides, fanaticism claimed its victims, while saints and men strong in their faith let the radiance of true humanity shine forth all the brighter. With the general break-up into factions, Europe's political unity also came to an end. The kingdom of Charles V, on which 'the sun never set', still claimed the universal authority of the Roman Empire; but national states now gradually asserted themselves, based on the absolute power of the ruler, who also determined his subjects' faith. Patrician republics were established in city states, like Venice, and in Holland. Spain, firmly united under Phillip II, ruler on two continents and a man of burning faith, became the leader of the Catholic party. With Austria, it predominated for a while, at the head of a united fleet defeated the Turks in the battle of Lepanto, but its Armada was in turn defeated off the shores of Britain and lost the Northern Netherlands. Meanwhile France, through the Hugenot wars, was brought to the brink of catastrophe, and Germany remained divided into two hostile religious camps. In Italy, freedom perished, the country was oppressed by foreign rule, and the Medici founded their dukedom on the ruins of the Florentine republic.

Despite all contacts with the surrounding world, Europe had so far lived within its own confines; now the earth became a tangible reality that had to be travelled, explored and finally conquered. This provided a further stimulus to movement and unrest. Indeed, even the very earth itself was moving around the sun. But how could this be compatible with the teachings of the Church? Giordano Bruno, who claimed that God dwelled in nature, ended at the stake, and Galileo was forced to recant. Yet the concept of the infinity of space, of a universe that maintains itself in constant movement, rapidly gained hold of man's consciousness. This collapse of the traditional picture of the world brought great upheaval; it was as if the very ground had yielded everywhere. The gaiety of the Renaissance paled, earnestness and speculative doubt spread everywhere, until a deep piety and intense discipline predominated in the Protestant camp no less than in the Catholic. Spanish fashion was adopted throughout: in the ruling circles, at the English and the French courts, life assumed a high degree of formalism and artificiality. Michelangelo, who suffered deeply from the religious conflicts of the age and the decline of his native city, out of melancholy found his way to faith and finally even renounced the creation of beautiful human form, ending his days as architect of St Peter's.

This phase of crisis and transition lasted from about 1530 to 1590, though it lingered into the new century in Germany; its art is called Mannerism.

The Age of the Baroque

Yet at the end of the sixteenth century the crisis was resolved: once more, a changed reality was accepted as a given fact. And now the Baroque world unfolded itself, a world of pulsating vigour and sublime spirituality, crude egoism and selfless devotion, full of the thunder of war and resounding festivity, of radiant spelendour and deep shadows, powerful and self-assured, hovering between day and twilit dream, dominated and formed by its own visionary concept. Mannerism had suffered from the conflict between this world and the next, between reality and the ideal; the Baroque experienced both as in a state of constant communion, and man himself, aware of his freedom and his roots in the Divine, shared in this all-transcending movement.

Baroque culture was rooted in a firmly ordered society. But, though each member was born into his class, personal achievement and free acquisition of property made social advancement easier, even to the ranks of nobility. The structure of society, still conceived as an allegory of universal harmony, was already assuming the social functions of the modern state. In Protestant as well as in Catholic countries, church and state now worked closely together; indeed, emphasis had gradually shifted to the secular realm. Since the second half of the sixteenth century, the Catholic Church, under powerful and militant popes, had placed everything, including the arts, into the service of the struggle; Mannerism, in the fullest sense, is the art of the Counter-reformation. Modelled on the church of Il Gesù in Rome, the type of the domed basilica, accompanied by the severe blocks of religious houses and filled with austere painting and sculpture, spread all over the Catholic world. But when the tension abated somewhat after the turn of the century and each religion fixed its limits clearly, the apparatus of propaganda became still more elaborate and psychologically sophisticated. Amidst the flow of light and the radiance of gold, ceiling frescoes and crowds of statues, the liturgy unfolded like a spectacle on the stage-like choir, and, through elaborate processions, the congregation was included, too, in the movement of a sacramental realm that extended, with its chapels and 'calvaries', far into the landscape. Protestantism, by its very nature, rejected such display: the more inward nature of its faith found expression in hymns and sacred music.

The all-pervading authority of the state was personified in the monarch. While Philip II still used Spain's religious mission as the justification of his royal will, Louis XIV equated his power with the demands of reason. Yet princely absolutism was more than a political institution. The office of the ruler was divinely ordained, entrusted with the task of keeping the universe in balance. Here, this world and the next, politics and religion, faith and reason, merged; the state as the mirror of the kingdom of God, and power as the means of its preservation, appeared sacred. Ancient concepts of the divine ruler lived on and permeated courtly allegory: the Emperor's ideal ancestry was traced via Augustus to Venus and Aeneas, Louis XIV called himself Apollo. The ruler not merely governed, but embodied, the state. This identification became manifest in the court ceremonial; originated in antiquity and remodelled in the Byzantine empire in the light of the Christian concept of Heaven, it had passed via Burgundy and Spain to the courts of Vienna and Versailles, which now served all Europe as example. Through symbolic gestures, the ceremonial transformed the life of the monarch and his court into the image of a higher existence.

The life of society was dominated by the example of the court. Dance, fashion, gesture and bearing followed the pattern laid down from above, the question of precedence assumed the utmost importance, sumptuary laws regulated degrees of display for each class, with particular severity in the Protestant countries. Even the relations between countries, politics and war, came to resemble a play that was acted in the European theatre according to fixed rules. Of course, the terrors of war and the sufferings of the peoples were in no way diminished; but though they were deplored and attempts were made to keep them in check, they still had their place in the order of Creation.

The eighteenth century, however, no longer believed in the magic of the great spectacle. The ceremonial appeared inconvenient, and the fashionable world escaped from it at every opportunity to 'maisons de plaisance', pavilions, and hermitages. In the Venetian carnival, the play between dream and reality came to a fascinating end, and, while the Revolution was already approaching, Marie Antoinette amused herself with a toy village. Rousseau replaced the beautiful illusion by another, in claiming that nature stood above form, indeed was almost synonymous with goodness. But, with the loss of the creative illusion, the power of the arts over life weakened.

Within the framework of its self-imposed order, the age passed through powerful historic events. Italy continued divided, Spain was in decline, whereas Holland experienced its greatest flowering. Germany, through the miseries of the Thirty Years' War, was thrown back fifty years. France, since Richelieu the best-governed, most populous and therefore most powerful country in Europe, developed an unsurpassed national culture that drew everything within its orbit: everyone now spoke French. Step by step, France's eastern border advanced, already the Empire was threatened, Strasburg fell, and the Turks stood at the gates of Vienna. But suddenly, the picture was reversed: a coalition held Louis XIV in check, and, in the wake of Prince Eugene's triumphs, Austria acquired the crown of Hungary and became a leading power. The split-up Empire revived, calm returned to Southern Germany, Brandenburg-Prussia rapidly developed into a leading power. Since Peter the Great, Russia had asserted herself increasingly, while Poland was broken up. Meanwhile England's maritime power had surpassed France and Holland; with the first signs of the coming revolution, the British Empire was gradually taking shape.

The Tasks of Sculpture

What were the tasks set to sculpture by that age, and how were they solved? Chief patrons were the Church, princely courts, the nobility and the middle class, which in the sixteenth century was still predominant in the city republics, but later on yielded to the nobility, except in Holland. The Catholic Church further unfolded its extensive artistic programme, and Anglicans and Lutherans, too, unlike Calvinists, admitted sculpture. Altar, pulpit, organ and choir stalls — in Spain, these extended far into the nave — were heaped with ornament. The predilection for devotional figures of every kind continued unabated; the South, in particular, loved processional groups and cribs. The relationship between sculpture and architecture appeared somewhat modified; walls and ceilings were populated by a multitude of figures, merged with the paintings that covered these surfaces. Here, *trompe l'œuil* was given free rein.

While the iconography of Church art still moved along the path laid down by tradition, secular sculpture, based on man's increased awareness of himself and on the cult of Classical antiquity, grew rapidly in importance. Monument, tomb and portrait, architectural sculpture and free-standing figures in palaces and gardens, as well as fountains in great diversity, yielded nothing in their importance to the sculpture of the church. Moreover, the border-line between sacred and profane was gradually fading. The Counter-reformation raised the Madonna to the top of the antique triumphal column, while the funeral monument increasingly brought the image of living man, with all the marks of his rank and character, into the interior of the church. The tomb is both sacred and profane; its very transcendentalism, its emphasis on the tension between life and death perfectly suited the mood of the age. Princes lay at rest in a mausoleum; others, according to rank and merit, were entitled to a free-standing tomb with or without a canopy, a wall tomb — found chiefly in Italy —, a memorial tablet, or just a modest stone slab in the floor.

Only the most exalted had an equestrian monument or were shown full length, while an innumerable number of portrait busts, particularly from the later sixteenth century, show characteristic likenesses of the time. The individualized portrait head of the Renaissance was less in vogue, whereas the portrait medal increasingly exploited the decorative qualities of wig and fashionable dress. Historical reliefs on monuments tell of the deeds of the great.

Apart from portrait and heroic biography, mythology is the dominant theme in secular sculpture. Allegories of powers and continents, of passions and destinies, vices and virtues, are predominantly given Classic form and appear — above all in Mannerism — as figures and groups, both as monumental statues and groups for display in palaces and squares, like the principal works of Cellini and Giambologna, and as small-scale figures for collectors. The allegoric representation and glorification of the ruler fills palace and park with a legion of mythological creatures; the staircase becomes the battleground of gods and titans, atlantes carry ceilings, cupids are everywhere. The garden becomes an ideal Arcadia, inhabited by nymphs and satyrs, threatened by monstrous faces; even a mountain god is raised in stone. In a grotto at Versailles, the king himself is portrayed as Apollo; while the horses of his sun-chariot are drinking, he rests among the muses from his triumphant journey. Water provides an infinite source of mythological interpretation, whether in parks or civic fountains. The delicate fountain groups of Mannerism, to be found mostly in Italy and Southern Germany, are followed by more ambitious schemes, in which the Baroque sense of mass and form achieves a unity of stone and bronze with the living element.

Even a fleeting survey shows that the Baroque sculpture was working within a clearly defined framework. The decoration of the church still remained the sculptor's chief concern, though profane architecture now equally availed itself of his services. Wherever the individual figure was intended to achieve a monumental effect, it sought a clear relationship to an open or enclosed space, to a square, arcaded hall, wall, or recess.

Meanwhile, from the Renaissance onwards, the work of art in its own right, independent of the greater ensemble, began on its journey as a piece of private property that could pass from hand to hand. This type of art, executed for the private patron, prefers the small or medium format, suitable for a domestic setting. The sixteenth century, in particular, loved the small figure, the elaborate and sophisticated form. The Baroque again preferred the sketch, the terracotta study, the promise of the unfinished, while the Rococo once more delighted in a diminutive world provided through the discovery of porcelain.

The Spread of the Baroque

The political changes of the time affected the flowering and the decline of the Baroque in each country. Italy, France, Germany and the Netherlands retained their importance. The Spanish and English contribution was in many respects comparable, despite the different national character; in both cases, alien elements were absorbed and transformed, though the mainstream of European development was hardly affected. This was also true of Scandinavia, while Saxony-Poland and Prussia, now closer to the heart of Europe, began to play an important part. Russia, after the sixteenth century, lived on an art imported from Central Europe, to which it gave its own cast. In America, Spanish and Portuguese Baroque and the classicism of England and the Netherlands gradually asserted themselves.

In the middle of the sixteenth century, Italy's reputation as the motherland of the arts, based on two-and-a-half centuries of outstanding activity, had reached its zenith. Michelangelo, venerated like a hero, was still alive; in architecture Palladio and Vignola were at the height of their powers; Venetian painting, with Veronese and Tintoretto, predominated. From the 'twenties, the basic concepts of Mannerist sculpture had been given distinct form, above all by Michelangelo in his Medici tombs and by masters like Cellini, Ammanati, and Bandinelli. The great artistic centre was Florence, where a Fleming, Jean de Boulogne — italicised as Giovanni da Bologna (Giambologna) — had established himself as the leading sculptor in the middle of the century and became the apostle of the new style. Pupils came from all over the world, while Italians, singly and in groups, accepted commissions throughout Europe. Thus the legacy of the Renaissance, transformed into Mannerism, crossed the Alps, not only as the style of the Counter-reformation in the art of the Church, but also as the new secular art of the courts and aristocracy everywhere. But very soon, this export art merged with local tradition, and international mannerism assumed national characteristics.

The first countries to fall within the orbit of the new style were France and Spain. Already around 1545, Goujon and Cousin mastered the new language, which they permeated with the delicate sense of line proper to French art since the Gothic. The principal master of the second half of the century was Germain Pilon, whose royal tombs of Saint-Denis, of an incomparable perfection of form, are the true successors of a vigorous native tradition. His art centred on the royal court. Italian masters, called to Spain by Philip II, soon adapted themselves to Spanish forms. Pompeo Leoni's tombs, amongst the most striking examples of later Mannerist sculpture, are essentially Spanish in character, while two Spanish artists, Berruguete and Juan de Juni, combine powerful Renaissance forms with their own Late Gothic craftsmanship in a life-size painted wooden sculpture of outstanding expressive power.

The so-called German Renaissance, too, at first was little more than a transition from Late Gothic forms to Mannerism; the general decline in the arts since the end of Dürer's age caused a noticeable void. New motifs, like counter-poise, still appear as purely decorative features in the carvings of Albert von Soest of c. 1570, in the figures on the Heidelberg Friedrichsbau, or in the Stuttgart Stiftskirche, where the Mannerist grouping in rows returns to the features of Gothic wall decoration. Towards 1580, though, the art of Giambologna gradually penetrated to Southern Germany, chiefly through Netherlandish masters like Hubert Gerhard and Adriaen de Vries, whose activity extended as far as Bohemia. In Holland, the turn of the century could still produce as great an achievement as the tomb of William of Orange, although sculpture was already taking second place to painting. Similarly in England, where Mannerism, adopted far more wholeheartedly than later the Baroque, passed through a highly original development in painting and lived on in sculpture, often in a somewhat provincial version, until well into the coming century.

At that time, Rome had already become the birthplace of the High Baroque, of the art of Bernini, his followers, and his adversaries. Architecture, sculpture and painting merged in an almost elemental outburst of activity. The very city, in the interplay of open spaces and massive blocks of architecture, became like the material in the sculptor's hand. Rome gave the outstanding example of modern town-planning; once again, Italy proved to be the teacher of all Europe.

VIII

After the middle of the century, this tutelage came to an end; national styles developed in great diversity. Rubens, in transforming the legacy of Rome and Venice, became the founder of Northern Baroque. His influence extended far beyond painting, it invigorated sculpture not only in the Netherlands, but all over Germany where, because of the Thirty Years' War, there was as yet little scope for original creative impulses. In Spain, on the other hand, painting flourished throughout a political decline while sculpture decreased in importance. In Holland, too, painting now far surpassed the other arts.

Foreign artists asserted themselves even in Rome, without adopting the Italian manner. Adam Elsheimer, Claude Lorrain and Nicolas Poussin did not become Italian painters; the latter, in particular, gave French art a new shape. But the turning point in the relationship between France and Italy came with the rejection of Bernini's design for the Louvre, submitted by the master himself on a visit to Paris in 1664. The prestige of French art, now generally acknowledged, was not so much based on the work of outstanding individuals as on the perfect balance through which it gave expression to the social order. The same balance is manifest in sculpture, in the light and measured step of the figures, in the distribution of ornament. Régence and Rococo then set the tone for a gayer and more intimate elegance. They are styles of ornament which penetrate all forms to such a degree that they have given their name to part of the eighteenth century; their decorative impulse also embraces a newly discovered material, porcelain. With the coming of the Classical revival, the arts are released from the predominance of ornament.

Many examples of English Baroque sculpture are either the work of artists from the Netherlands or show foreign influence. Many a striking portrait bust reflects a strong sense of individuality. Like the Netherlands and Spain, England's chief contribution in the eighteenth century lies in painting.

Germany is the country of late styles, of the synthesis of the achievements of the surrounding nations. Since the Thirty Years' War, foreigners had led in the arts — Italians in the South, Flemings, Dutchmen and French refugees in the North-west and the North. Now, in the course of political consolidation in the 'nineties of the seventeenth century, the great age of the German Baroque began with the appearance of Fischer von Erlach in Vienna and Schlüter in Berlin. The main emphasis was on architecture and sculpture; painting was reduced to little more than the decoration of walls and ceilings. Schlüter and Fischer, like Rubens before them, transplanted the Italian High Baroque into their native soil, which responded with a long-dormant fertility. At a second stage, Italian plasticity combined with the teachings of French art, and German architecture thus assumed a truly European character. Radiating from Austria, it triumphed throughout Germany, attaining its highest perfection in the interiors of Balthasar Neumann and his companions. Late German Baroque sculpture was an integral part of this architecture.

The Character and Development of Style

Styles are accepted terms used to describe in retrospect certain developments in the history of art. Specific traits emerge, and a basis is created for some kind of understanding, particulary if we remember that a form of art always expresses some relationship to reality.

Mannerism experienced this relationship as disturbed, questionable, marked by conflict. This mood was also expressed in the interpretation of the most important legacy of the High Renaissance, the human form, at first still rendered in life-like proportions according to the canons of Antiquity with even movement carefully balanced in counter-poise. The figures in Michelangelo's Sistine chapel still follow this tradition. In the master's Medici, however, the bodies are already elongated, their muscles unnaturally accentuated. Their floating movement appears like an expression of the struggle against some heavy paralysing force. Beauty seems steeped in melancholy. In Cellini's 'Perseus', these beginnings, developed to perfection, have matured into the dominant style. Between youthful splendour and the grimness of death lies the abyss of earthly existence, above which the power of form holds an overshadowed dream world in balance.

Yet such cool and severely remote perfection expresses spiritual conflict, passions and desires, no less than the freedom of Renaissance forms, though no warmth streams from it. Art altogether now loses the unselfconsciousness it has inherited from the crafts. It becomes aware of its specific nature, of its self-sufficiency; the door is opened to its existence in its own right, to its modern interpretation. When reality has become questionable, art must recreate and affirm it in its own realm, a process that is only possible in a state of tension. Here lies the root of the Mannerist conflict. The figure creates its own space against its surroundings, indeed, space itself becomes the subject of expression. This introverted ideal appears perfectly in the *figura serpentinata* of the Italians, above all in Giambologna's sculpture. A single figure, or, better still, a group of figures, forms a spiral-like, contorted composition, which offers innumerable aspects, though no frontal view. The whole scheme moves around its own axis, almost painfully close to life, yet forever remote; its relationship to the beholder is broken and problematic. An effort is needed to enter its reality.

This compulsion of form also governs Landini's '*Fontana dei Tartarughe*' in Rome. The graceful youths are arranged in pairs; Mannerism loves the dualism that confuses a given object with its reflection. The slender limbs wind into an ornament that, basket-like, surrounds the space where this charm unfolds. The element of water, too, must not flow naturally; pressed into pipes, it sprays up and downwards in thin rays that become part of the linear design. Beauty is magic, ever present yet intangible. Reality is never shown outright in this style; it only arises out thesis and antithesis. Life, too, only attains completion through the confrontation with death. Below the canopy where Germain Pilon's royal couple kneels in full majesty, the same royal figures appear as naked corpses.

This concept was not new, and in France medieval feeling lived on rather more than in Italy, where Mannerism toyed with death in innumerable allegories while avoiding the ultimate truth. The formal, over-loaded dress was entirely in keeping with this coercion of the living form. Copied in every detail, the dress became a formal element of its own, through which the body is merely indicated. English Late Renaissance tombs in particular portray an almost explosive tension of remoteness and life-like realism. Perhaps this expresses an essentially English element, just as the crudeness of suffering within a frozen diagram of lines in Fernandez' groups may seem characteristically Spanish. Feelings and forms which had existed side by side in medieval art broke into contrast under a sharpening consciousness; the mastery of such contrasts now increasingly became the mission of form.

The Baroque, unlike Mannerism, presupposed a straightforward emotional relationship of the beholder to the world of art. Italian painting had radically restored this way of approach around 1590. The fresco of the Carracci covers walls and ceilings with powerful, deceivingly life-like figures; Caravaggio, in rendering biblical scenes as natural events unfolding before an audience, achieves in his altarpiece unity of action and persuasive power. These masters have created the basis of the Roman High Baroque. Bernini's 'Neptune and Triton', an early work, appears at first sight little different in its composition from Giambologna's 'Samson and the Philistine'; yet the group, no longer contorted, reveals itself in a frontal view. The same metamorphosis is evident from comparison of two, admittedly less important, works of Francheville, separated by the decisive decade. In Bernini's 'Apollo and Daphne' the marble has been endowed with the illusion of pulsating life, the fleeting moment of transformation seems to have been made tangible. Religious sculpture of the time shows every degree of expression, from silent contemplation to visionary ecstasy. 'The Ecstasy of St Theresa of Avila' is a full-figured altar group. The miracle takes place above the clouds, framed by a pillared doorway and lit up from a hidden source, with the donors turning towards it from their boxes on both sides like spectators in a theatre. The worshipper feels himself part of the whole scene; stage and auditorium merge into one transcendental reality. This scenic interpretation affects all the visual arts: tombs show the deceased collapsing, in prayer, or in life-like gestures like that of the blessing pope, and subsidiary figures, hitherto of purely allegoric or formal significance, share in the general unity of action. Thus death opens the gate of the tomb below the kneeling Alexander VII, or enters the name of the dead in his book, as on Schlüter's sarcophagus of the Queen of Prussia. The portrait seeks a high degree of individual likeness and, despite all the discipline of form, exploits to the utmost the whole range of emotional tension. But this wealth of expression is not confined to the face. Bernini brings the dress to life, allowing it, as in medieval art, to break through the barriers of its natural flow so that it becomes the vehicle of a spiritual message, without losing any of its material quality.

The draperies flow round the figure, are gathered up together in tension, ascend, or collapse, trembling with the last dying breath. Their effect is heightened when they are made of coloured material. The fountains marry water, light, and stone in highly picturesque scenic compositions, like Bernini's 'Four River Fountain' or the later 'Fontana di Trevi'. While Mannerism enclosed the dark-glowing bronze figure in a network of sprays, the element now runs in free flow yet still guided, and surrounds the marble-white bodies of the water deities like liquid draperies.

The expansive, yet entirely human, gesture of the Italian Baroque found no lasting response in Spain, although sculpture, as in the case of Pereyra or Cano, did pass through this particular stylistic phase. A silent though inwardly burning figure like Pedro de Mena's 'St Francis' seems more suited to the Spanish character. Later, a popular type of devotional groups nearly exceeded the limits of art by their imitative naturalism animated by violent emotion.

In France, however, the full range of the High Baroque was adopted, though sobered down to greater clarity and a more rational order. The court art of Louis XIV, managed by Colbert and Lebrun, kept an even standard of high quality; Girardon and Coyzevaux, like Coustou and Bouchardon later on, were masters of the first order, though never outstanding. Puget, who, as an outsider, took his own path from Hellenism and Bernini to intense pathos and dramatic grouping, was the only genius among the French sculptors of the time. Tomb figures like Coyzevaux' Colbert or Guérin's are unthinkable without Roman Baroque, yet they appear more reserved in their expression, restrained in their draperies, though the likeness is more marked; indeed, French portrait sculpture developed brilliantly and left an eloquent picture of the outstanding personalities of the *Grand Siècle*. Girardon in particular, reflects the Classic taste that is so marked in French architecture and gives the whole intellectual life of the country its distinct flavour. Again and again, Italian concepts are given a French interpretation. Thus Bouchardon's *Fontaine de Grenelle* is a translation of Michelangelo's Medici tombs, complete with naturalistic detail in the manner of Bernini, into Classic two-dimensionality, bearing and dress. Classicism, already established as early as 1740, does not allow the development of true Rococo sculpture. Pigalles's 'Mercury' of 1748 gives another example of its apparition besides borrowing some motifs from the ceiling of the Sistine Chapel. The same master's Harcourt monument, as late as 1774, still adheres to a High Baroque setting, which, however, is split into two relief layers according to Classic rules. The scenery is fashioned *à l'antique* and somewhat sentimentalized, thus dissolving the unity of content and form Bernini had never given up, into a dissonance of reality and ideal. The Nightingale tomb, by Roubillac, is an even more notable example of the same tendency on English soil. The inherited form no longer corresponds to the new conception of reality already determined by the philosophy of enlightenment.

On German soil, like everywhere north of the Alps, the effect of the crisis of *c.* 1590 in Italian sculpture was, at first, mirrored only indirectly in the different local versions of Late Mannerism. However, Germany was placed geographically between the Italian Early Baroque and the art of Rubens. Ekbert Wolf's Bückeburg Golden Hall, Jörg Zürn's Late Gothic altarpiece at Überlingen and, since the second decade of the new century, the imported art of Adriaen de Vries show an increasing tendency towards heavier forms of a plainer appearance. Münstermann, in the north, appears like a last upholder of Later Mannerism with works reminiscent of El Greco. In Reichle's Augsburg 'St Michael' group and in Krumper's powerful tomb of Ludwig the Bavarian, forms have considerably relaxed, though some of the rigidity of Mannerism remains. In the Regensburg 'Mary Magdalen' of 1625, attributed to Petel, it is completely transcended; the draperies flow naturally, feeling utters itself without restraint, yet, after the Thirty Years' War, Gleskher's Bamberg group remained an isolated example; the whole development seemed to be fading out. Reflections of the High Baroque did not appear until about 1675, for instance with Rauchmiller's art at Trèves, probably based on French models, in the highly individual work of the younger Zürn at Kremsmünster and, translated back into a post-Gothic idiom, in Schwanthaler's sculpture in the Salzburg region. But so far there were no signs of an emancipation from the surrounding countries.

The picture changed around 1690. Unlike in France, the Late Baroque in Germany gained ground through the work of eminent masters; with a rigorous start, the delay of half a century was made good.

The turning point came with Schlüter, the heir of Michelangelo and Bernini, Germany's greatest sculptor, and, indeed around 1700 the outstanding sculptural power in Europe. His art sums up the achievements of Italy, the Netherlands and France, and makes the art of Antiquity his own. Favoured by historical conditions, he creates with the key-stones of the Berlin Arsenal, the figures in and outside the Berlin Schloss, the royal tombs and the Homburg bust works of such perfection of form, expressive power and poetic profundity that a completely new standard is set in Germany. His fame is assured, above all, by his equestrian statue of the Great Elector, where, attaining a degree of mastery comparable only to Antiquity and Donatello, he has achieved a synthesis of Rome, the Renaissance and the age of Louis XIV. Schlüter's work strikes the final chord of the High Baroque and therefore remains without immediate succession, though its indirect effect is considerable. Permoser, who transformed the façades of the Dresden Zwinger into sculpture, was governed by its mighty impulse.

Austrian and South German sculpture of the eighteenth century, in its infinite diversity, was entirely dependent on given settings, whether as ornament of church and altar or of secular buildings, parks and squares, street and bridges; its influence extended towards West, North and East, as far as Poland and Hungary. Apart from stone, stucco and metal, painted and gilded wood were favourite materials. Woodcarving was an old German tradition, never extinct though at times dormant. Now it flowered in magnificent profusion, still rooted in the crafts though attaining European rank with examples like Ignaz Günther's Annunciation group. This is a work very different from the contemporary Classic revival in West and South, which can be compared in the Montagu tomb at Warkton, and which was to determine the future concept of sculpture so completely that the German Late Baroque came to be almost forgotten. Günther is not concerned with *contraposto* but with figures floating in space, not with the tangible mass but with visual effects. The roots of his art lead both to Bernini and back to the Middle Ages. Almost unnoticeably, the Classic canons are abandoned even by the Italians working in the North around 1725. Carlone's Joachim at Weingarten illustrates this clearly by comparison with Rusconi's 'St Matthew' in S. Giovanni in Laterano; he stands firmly implanted on the ground, but his draperies are like a denial of the solidity of matter. Feuchtmayer, in his Überlingen St Christopher, has gone further; here, a Herculean figure has become completely subordinate to the flowing line derived from old German woodcuts and engravings. The master's graceful Virgin of the Annunciation, too, forms an ornament that is both a Gothic S-curve and a coloured *rocaille*. Yet this makes her concern at the heavenly message in no way appear less pure and genuine.

Bernini's concept of scenography, based on the synthesis of the various arts, proved nowhere more fertile than in German church architecture. The interiors of Weltenburg and Rohr, created by the Asam brothers, amidst the radiance of gold and colours, changed into the serene spectacle of the *theatrum sacrum:* altar is turned into stage. The narrow interior of St Nepomuk's at Munich, by the same masters, seems to rise from the ground; Dürer's 'Mercy Seat', translated into sculpture, hovers high above the altar. But the full range of the work of this generation only becomes revealed in the work of Georg Raphael Donner. In complete contrast to the illusionist art of the Asam brothers, the Austrian master's altars and fountains, cast in silvery lead, are composed of figures of Classic harmony and balance.

Meanwhile the trend towards a hidden Gothic revival continued. Interiors were laid over with figures and ornament in such a way that they seem to surge in storm, to undulate. Gold and the heavier colours were replaced by white. In the Bavarian Wieskirche, saints flutter along the walls like butterflies, bathed in light. In secular art, whether among the Classic deities in the Würzburg Kaisersaal, in garden sculpture or in porcelain — which attains its highest perfection in groups inspired by Venetian comedy —, the figure willingly surrenders to the gaiety of dance. Nor does a reduced scale mean a loss of dramatic effect, as the silver figure of the Elector Maximilian Joseph at Altötting proves.

A gentle ecstasy pervades Joseph Christian's graceful saints and angels, a more vigorous note is struck by Thaddaeus Stammel, who has illustrated the Dance of Death in his library at Admont; the same medieval motifs, almost as if touched by the mood of the medieval bishops' tombs, occurs amidst the already Classic décor of the convent church at Salem. Feeling and form show an unbroken vitality, free from the kind of affectation which occurs in contemporary French funeral statuary. But soon afterwards, the effect of Winkelmann's writings was to put an end to this late flowering of the Baroque.

Werner Hager

INDEX OF SCULPTORS

With his late work, Michelangelo, the outstanding genius of the High Renaissance
and the father of the Baroque, becomes also the creator of Mannerism, the style between the
two epochs. *Milan*. Museo Civico. The uncompleted Pietà from the Rondanini collection.

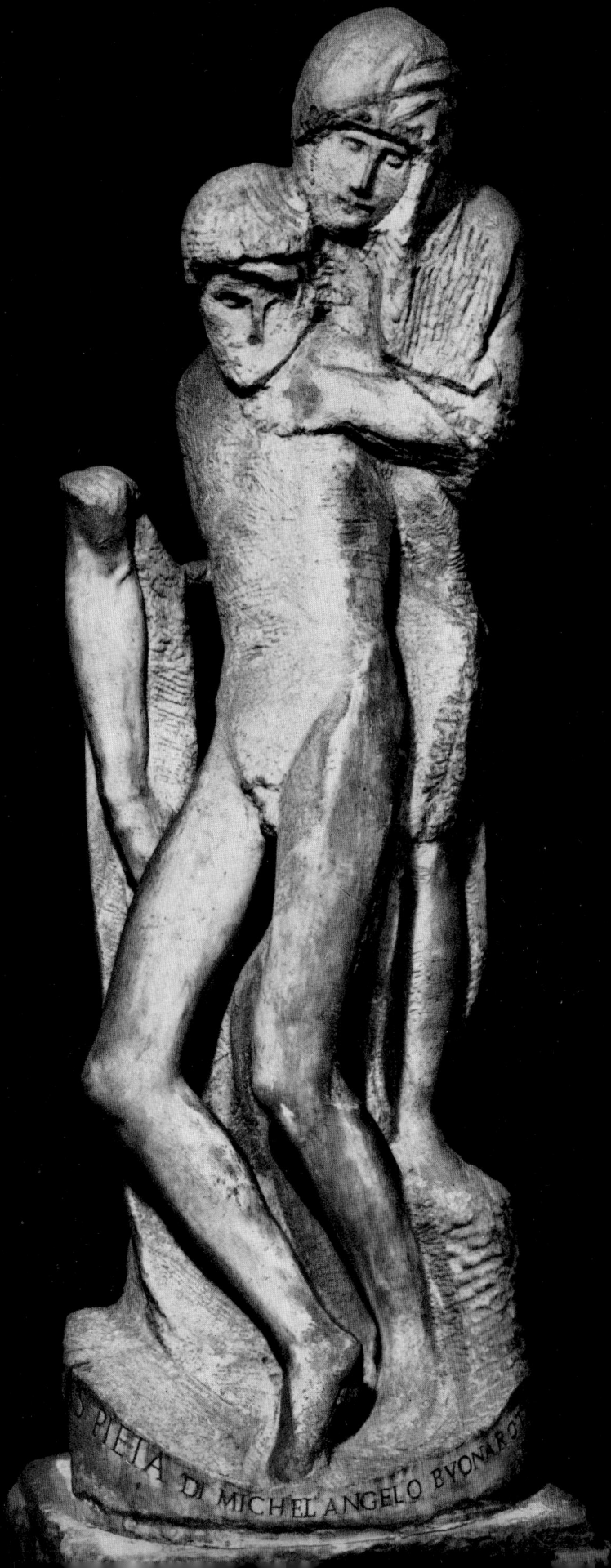

PIETA DI MICHEL ANGELO BVONAROTI

Roubier

Neben die selbstsichere Schönheit der Renaissancekunst tritt im Manierismus eine verhaltene Trauer — bis zu Lebensangst und Grauen. *Florenz*.
Loggia dei Lanzi. Perseus-Statue. 1553, von Benvenuto Cellini. Bronze. Oben: Perseus mit dem Haupt der Medusa. Rechts: Danae mit dem Knaben Perseus, vom Sockel des Standbilds.

In Mannerism, the self-assured beauty of the Renaissance gradually yields to a restrained sorrow, accentuated at times to fear and despair. *Florence*.
Loggia dei Lanzi. Perseus. 1553, by Benvenuto Cellini. Bronze. Above: Perseus with the head of Medusa. Right: Danae with the boy Perseus, from the base.

MAS

Aus dem Studium der Natur, charakteristisch schon für Spätgotik und Renaissance, erwachsen in Spanien bewegte Formen, in Frankreich dagegen stille von höfisch-klassischem Ernst. Auf dieser Seite: *Paris.* Louvre. Zwei Beweinungen Christi. Oben: 1545, von Jean Goujon. Darunter: Über das Vorbild Goujons hinausgewachsen: das Werk von Germain Pilon. 1585. Rechts: *Toledo.* Kathedrale. Eva am Chorgestühl. 1543, von Alonso Berruguete.

In Spain, the study of nature, characteristic already of the Late Gothic and the Renaissance, inspires greater movement, in France a calm and courtly Classic. On this page: *Paris.* Louvre. Two Lamentations, above, 1545, by Jean Goujon, and, below, by Germain Pilon (1585), who has transcended Goujon's example. Right: *Toledo.* Cathedral. Eve, from the choir stalls. 1543, by Alonso Berruguete.

4

Foto Marburg/Archives Photographiques

Die „figura serpentinata" des Manierismus zeigt langgestreckte, in reichem Richtungswechsel sich windende Gestalten, hier von feinem Faltenwerk umspielt. Links: *Paris*. Louvre. Quellnymphe von der „Fontaine des Innocents". 1549, von Jean Goujon. Mitte: *Paris*. Louvre. Genius mit gesenkter Fackel vom Grabmal des Philippe de Jabot. Um 1550, von Jean Cousin. Oben: *Rom*. S. Pietro in Montorio. Grabmal des Antonio del Monte. 1553–54, von Bartolomeo Ammanati.

Here, the *figura serpentinata* of Mannerism, elongated and contorted in many directions, is enveloped in the gentle ripple of the draperies. Left: *Paris*. Louvre. Fountain nymph from the 'Fontaine des Innocents." 1549, by Jean Goujon. Centre: *Paris*. Louvre. Standing figure with lowered torch from the tomb of Philippe de Jabot. C. 1550, by Jean Cousin. Above: *Rome*. S. Pietro in Montorio. Tomb of Antonio del Monte. 1553–1554, by Bartolomeo Ammanati.

Die Liniensprache des Manierismus verbindet sinnlichen Naturalismus mit Eleganz der Bewegung, häufig auch mit schmerzlicher Gebärde.
Oben: *Berlin*. Staatliche Museen. Modell für eine Brunnenfigur. Um 1550, von Giovanni Angelo Montorsoli. Rechts: *Rom*. Piazza Mattei.
Der Schildkrötenbrunnen. 1585, von Taddeo Landini.

The language of the Mannerist line combines sensuality and realism with graceful movement, often also with the expression of anguish and sorrow.
Above: *Berlin*. Staatliche Museen. Bozzetto for a fountain figure. C. 1550, by Giovanni Montorsoli. Right: *Rome*. Piazza Mattei. Fontana delle Tartarughe.
1585, by Taddeo Landini.

Hell

Bewegte Haltung und sorgfältige Wiedergabe der
Anatomie kennzeichnen eine frühbarocke Phase im Norden,
in der auch spätgotische Tradition nachlebt.
Links: *Tübingen*. Stiftskirche. Medaillon mit Gottvater und
Christus am Grabmal Herzog Ulrichs (gestorben 1550).
Von Josef Schmid aus Urach.
Rechts: *Paris*. Louvre. Auferstandener Christus. Um 1580,
von Germain Pilon.

Animated gesture and careful attention to anatomic detail
are characteristic of a Northern Early Baroque,
in which the Late Gothic tradition lives on.
Left: *Tübingen*. Convent Church. Medallion with God
the Father and Christ, from the tomb of Duke Ulrich
(d. 1550). By Josef Schmid of Urach.
Right: *Paris*. Louvre. Risen Christ. C. 1580,
by Germain Pilon.

Foto Marburg

Carvajal

MAS

Gesteigerter Verismus bei übersteigerter Ausdrucksbewegung von Körper, Antlitz und Gewand charakterisiert die Werke von Juan de Juni,
der in Spanien die Spätgotik in den Manierismus führt. Oben: *Valladolid*. Museo Nacional de Escultura. Maria und Johannes von einer Beweinung Christi.
1541/44. Rechts: *Valladolid*. Iglesia de las Angustias. Die „Virgen de los Chuchillos". Um 1560.

Body, face and dress are of an almost exaggerated expressive power in the work of Juan de Juni, whose art forms the transition from Spanish Late Gothic to
Mannerism. Above: *Valladolid*. Museo Nacional de Escultura. Mary and St. John, from a Lamentation. 1541/44. Right: *Valladolid*. Iglesia de las Angustias.
The "Virgen de los Chuchillos." C. 1560.

Die Grabmäler des Franzosen Germain Pilon sind Sinnbilder weltschmerzlicher, aber höfisch gefaßter Haltung. Ihr Stil wird maßgeblich für die französische Kunst. Links oben: *Paris.* Louvre. Grabmal der Valentine Balbiani als Ruhende und als Leichnam. (Gestorben 1572.) Darunter: *St. Denis.* Grabmal Heinrichs II. und der Katharina Medici. 1570. Oben: Detail vom Grabmal der Valentine Balbiani.

The funeral monuments of Germain Pilon are images of grief controlled by courtly bearing. Their style was to become decisive in French art. Left, above: *Paris.* Louvre. Tomb of Valentine Balbiani (d. 1572), who is shown in life and in death. Below: *St. Denis.* Tomb of Henry II and Catherine Medici. 1570. Above: detail from the tomb of Valentine Balbiani.

Im Bildnis lebt die große Tradition der Renaissance weiter, bereichert um tieferes Verständnis des Psychologischen. Oben: *Paris*. Louvre. Cabinet des Médailles. Medaille mit dem Kopf Heinrich II. Von Germain Pilon. Detail. Rechts: *Accum bei Wilhelmshaven*. Pfarrkirche. Kopf der Eva von Renneberg von ihrem Grabmal. 1567. Unbekannter Meister. Schwarzer Marmor.

The great tradition of the Renaissance lives on in the portrait, enriched by a more profound understanding of the psychological element. Above: *Paris*. Louvre. Cabinet des Médailles. Medal with the head of Henry II (detail). By Germain Pilon. Right: *Accum nr. Wilhelmshaven*. Parish **Church**. Head of Eva von Renneberg, from her tomb. 1567. Unknown master. Black marble.

16

Freistehende Brunnen bilden städtebauliche Akzente. *Bologna*. Detail vom Neptunsbrunnen. 1563–1567, von Giovanni da Bologna.

Free-standing fountains as the focal points of towns. *Bologna*. Detail from the Neptune fountain. 1563–1567, by Giovanni da Bologna.

Manieristisch-dünnstrahlig spritzen die Wasserspiele der Brunnen. *Nürnberg*. Detail vom Tugendbrunnen. 1585–1589, von Benedikt Wurzelbauer.

Nuremberg. Detail from the Tugendbrunnen. 1585–1589, by Benedikt Wurzelbauer.

Raichle

Bologna. Piazza del Nettuno. Harpyie vom Neptunsbrunnen (siehe S. 18). 1563–1567, von Giovanni da Bologna.

Bologna. Piazza del Nettuno. Figure from the Neptune fountain (q. v. ill. 18). 1563–67, by Giovanni da Bologna.

Florenz. Piazza della Signoria. Detail vom Neptunsbrunnen. 1569–75, von Bartolomeo Ammanati.

Florence. Piazza della Signoria. Detail from the Neptune fountain. 1569–75, by Bartolomeo Ammanati.

Giovanni da Bologna,
ein Flame aus Boulogne, wird
zum virtuosen Hauptmeister des
Manierismus in Florenz.
Seine Gestalten sind für die
Betrachtung von allen Seiten
entworfen.
Links: *London*. Victoria and
Albert Museum. Samson und
der Philister. 1568.
Rechts: *Florenz*. Venus von der
„Fontana di Donzella" im
Garten des Palazzo Pitti.
Um 1580.

Giovanni da Bologna, a Fleming
from Boulogne, becomes the
brilliant principal master
of Mannerism in Florence. His
figures are designed to be
seen from all sides.
Left: *London*. Victoria and
Albert Museum. Samson and
the Philistine. 1568.
Right: *Florence*. Venus, from
the "Fontana di Donzella" in the
gardens of the Palazzo Pitti.
C. 1580.

Der Niederländer Hubert
Gerhard verpflanzt den Stil
des Giovanni da Bologna nach
Süddeutschland. *München*.
Bavaria von der Kuppel des
Tempelchens im Hofgarten
(ursprünglich als Diana für
einen Brunnen bestimmt).
Bronze. 1623.

Hubert Gerhard, from the
Netherlands, transplants the
style of Giovanni da Bologna to
Southern Germany. *Munich*.
The Bavaria figure from the
cupola of the small temple in
the Hofgarten (intended
originally as a figure of Diana
for a fountain). Bronze. 1623.

Dülberg

Selbst auf religiösen Kunstwerken erscheinen jetzt blühend sinnliche Gestalten in modisch geschraubter Haltung. *Soest.* St. Patroklus. Fuß eines Vortragekreuzes. Um 1600, von dem Silberschmied Anton Eisenhoit.

Even in religious art, figures of a glowing sensuality, fashionably contorted, now appear. *Soest, Westphalia.* St. Patroklus. Base of a processional cross. C. 1600, by the silversmith Anton Eisenhoit.

Windstoßer

Im Manierismus lebt noch einmal eine Welt des Dämonischen auf. Oben: *Pratolino bei Florenz*. „Der Apennin" aus dem Park der Villa Medici. 1577/81, von Giovanni da Bologna. Rechts: *Bomarzo bei Viterbo*. Felsenplastik im „Sacro Bosco" des Orsinischlosses. Um 1560, wahrscheinlich von Bartolomeo Ammanati.

A demonic world comes to life once more in Mannerism. Above: *Pratolino near Florence*. The Apennine figure from the park of the Villa Medici. 1577/81, by Giovanni da Bologna. Right: *Bomarzo near Viterbo*. Rock sculpture in the "Sacro Bosco" of the Orsini palace. C. 1560, probably by Bartolomeo Ammanati.

26

Satyrn, Höllenfürsten und verwandte Gestalten in äußerstem Realismus der Physiognomik. Links: *München*. Bayerisches Nationalmuseum. Satyrmaske. Elfenbein. Um 1625, von Christoph Angermair. Oben: *Augsburg*. Zeughaus. Luzifer von der bronzenen Michaelsgruppe an der Fassade. 1602—07, von Hans Reichle. Detail.

Satyrs, princes of hell and related figures, shown with expressions of the utmost realism. Left: *Munich*. Bayerisches Nationalmuseum. Satyr's mask. C. 1625, by Christoph Angermair. Ivory. Above: *Augsburg*. Zeughaus. Lucifer, from the bronze St. Michael's group on the façade (detail). 1602—07, by Hans Reichle.

29

Lüneburg. Große Ratsstube.
Teil einer Türrahmung: Darius
und Temperantia. 1566—84,
von Albert von Soest.

Lüneburg. Great Council
Chamber. Part of a door
surround. Darius and
Temperantia. 1566—85, by Albert
von Soest.

Boy-Schmidt   30

R. Müller

Das in der Renaissance erwachsene Selbstbewußtsein führt nun bis zu Eitelkeit und Überladung in Kleidermode und Rüstung. *Stuttgart*. Chor der Stiftskirche. Gedenkplastiken für die Grafen von Württemberg. 1574, von Simon Schlör.

Self-awareness, which gradually emerged during the Renaissance, is now carried to the point of vanity and exaggeration in dress and armour. *Stuttgart*. Convent church. The monuments to the Counts of Württemberg in the choir. 1574, by Simon Schlör.

England ist besonders reich an Grabmälern der Zeit um 1600, die Einblick in Familienleben und Tracht der Epoche geben.
Oben: *Stow-Nine-Churches, Northants*. Grabmal der Lady Elizabeth Carey. 1617, von Nicholas Stone.
Rechts: *Gloucester*. Kathedrale. Grabmal der Elizabeth Williams. Vor 1600.

England is particularly rich in monuments of the time round 1600; many of these afford an insight into the family life and fashions of the period.
Above: *Stow-Nine-Churches, Northants*. Tomb of Lady Elizabeth Carey. 1617, by Nicholas Stone.
Right: *Gloucester*. Cathedral. Tomb of Elizabeth Williams. Pre 1600.

Busch

Blütezeit dekorativer Ausstattung im Manierismus, dessen „horror vacui" oft zur Überfülle führt. Links: *Weikersheim*. Schloß. Kamin im Rittersaal. Um 1600, von Michael Junker. Oben: *Münster i. W.* Dom. Epitaph des Otto v. Dorgelo. 1614, von Melchior Kribbe.

Flowering of the decorative arts in Mannerism, whose "horror vacui" frequently leads to exuberance and overloading. Left: *Weikersheim, Württemberg*. Castle. Fireplace in the Rittersaal. C. 1600, by Michael Junker. Above: *Münster, Westphalia*. Cathedral. Epitaph of Otto von Dorgelo. 1614, by Melchior Kribbe.

Busch

In Norddeutschland gewinnt ein später Manierismus erschütternde Aussagekraft. In verkrampften Körpern bekunden sich die zwiespältigen Lüste und Ängste der Epoche, die durch den 30jährigen Krieg gekennzeichnet ist. Oben: *Paderborn*. Dom. Fürstenberg-Epitaph. Ausschnitt aus dem Jüngsten Gericht. Um 1620, von Heinrich Gröninger. Rechts: *Oldenburg*. Landesmuseum. Adam und Eva. Bruchstück eines Taufsteindeckels aus Holle. Holz. 1623, von Ludwig Münstermann.

In Northern Germany, Late Mannerism attains a deeply moving expressive power. Cramped and contorted bodies reflect the desires and fears of an epoch marked by the Thirty Years' War. Above: *Paderborn*. Cathedral. Fürstenberg epitaph. Detail from the Last Judgement. C. 1620, by Heinrich Gröninger. Right: *Oldenburg*. Landesmuseum. Adam and Eve. Fragment of the cover of a font formerly at Holle. Wood. 1623, by Ludwig Münstermann.

36

Die expressionistische Formgebung Ludwig Münstermanns nimmt in manchem um 1600 bereits Züge des Rokoko vorweg.
Bremen. Fockemuseum. Engelskopf vom Orgelprospekt aus Rotenburg. Holz. 1608.

The expressionism of Ludwig Münstermann's art anticipates some Rococo traits as early as the beginning of the seventeenth century. *Bremen.* Fockemuseum. Angel's head, from an organ prospect, formerly in Rotenburg. Wood. 1608.

Busch

Bremen. Fockemuseum. Kopf einer Herkulesfigur von einer Bremer Hausfassade. Sandstein. Um 1600, von Ludwig Münstermann.
Bremen. Fockemuseum. Head of a figure of Hercules from a Bremen façade. Sandstone. C. 1600, by Ludwig Münstermann.

Der Hof zu *Bückeburg* bildet den verheißungsvollen Mittelpunkt eines eigenständigen Kunstschaffens, das mit dem 30jährigen Krieg jäh abbrach.
Oben: Schloßkapelle. Engel als Träger des Altartisches. Ausschnitt. 1601–14, von Ekbert Wolf d. J. Rechts: „Goldener Saal" des Schlosses. „Venus" von der Göttertür. 1605, von Ekbert Wolf d. J.

The court at *Bückeburg*, promising centre of an indigenous art that was to come to an abrupt end with the Thirty Years' War. Above: the chapel. Angels as supports of an altar table. Detail. 1601–14, by Ekbert Wolf the younger. Right: "Golden Hall" of the castle. "Venus", from the "portal of the gods". 1605, by Ekbert Wolf the younger.

Foto Marburg/Roubier

In den Niederlanden herrscht
Realismus bis zur Darstellung selbst des
Krankhaften — in Frankreich
Idealisierung bis hin zur Pose.
Gemeinsam ist die zeitgebundene
„Schraubung" der Gestalt.
Links: *Amsterdam*. Rijksmuseum. Eine
Irre. Sandstein, überlebensgroß.
Anf. 17. Jh., von Geraert Lambertsz.
Rechte Seite: *Paris*. Louvre. Werke von
Pierre Francheville. Links: David mit
dem Haupt des Goliath. 1608.
Rechts: Orpheus. 1598.

In the Netherlands, realism, carried
even to the representation of the
pathological — in France, idealisation
accentuated to affectation; the sculpture
of both countries shows the same
contortion of the figure.
Left: *Amsterdam*. Rijksmuseum.
A madwoman. Sandstone, larger than
life. Early 17th century, by
Geraert Lambertsz.
Right page: *Paris*. Louvre. Two works
by Pierre Francheville. Left: David with
the head of Goliath. 1608.
Right: Orpheus. 1598.

Rijksmuseum Amsterdam 42

MAS

In Spanien ist Pompeo Leoni der Meister repräsentativer Fürstengräber. Links: *El Escorial*. Monument für Karl V. Um 1600. Oben: *Salas, Asturien*. Colegiata.
Grabmal des Großinquisitors Fernando de Valdés, Erzbischof von Sevilla. Um 1600.

In Spain, Pompeo Leoni is the outstanding master of the princely funeral monument. Left: *El Escorial*. Tomb of Charles V. C. 1600.
Above: *Salas, Asturia*. Colegiata. Tomb of Fernando de Valdés, archbishop of Sevilla. C. 1600.

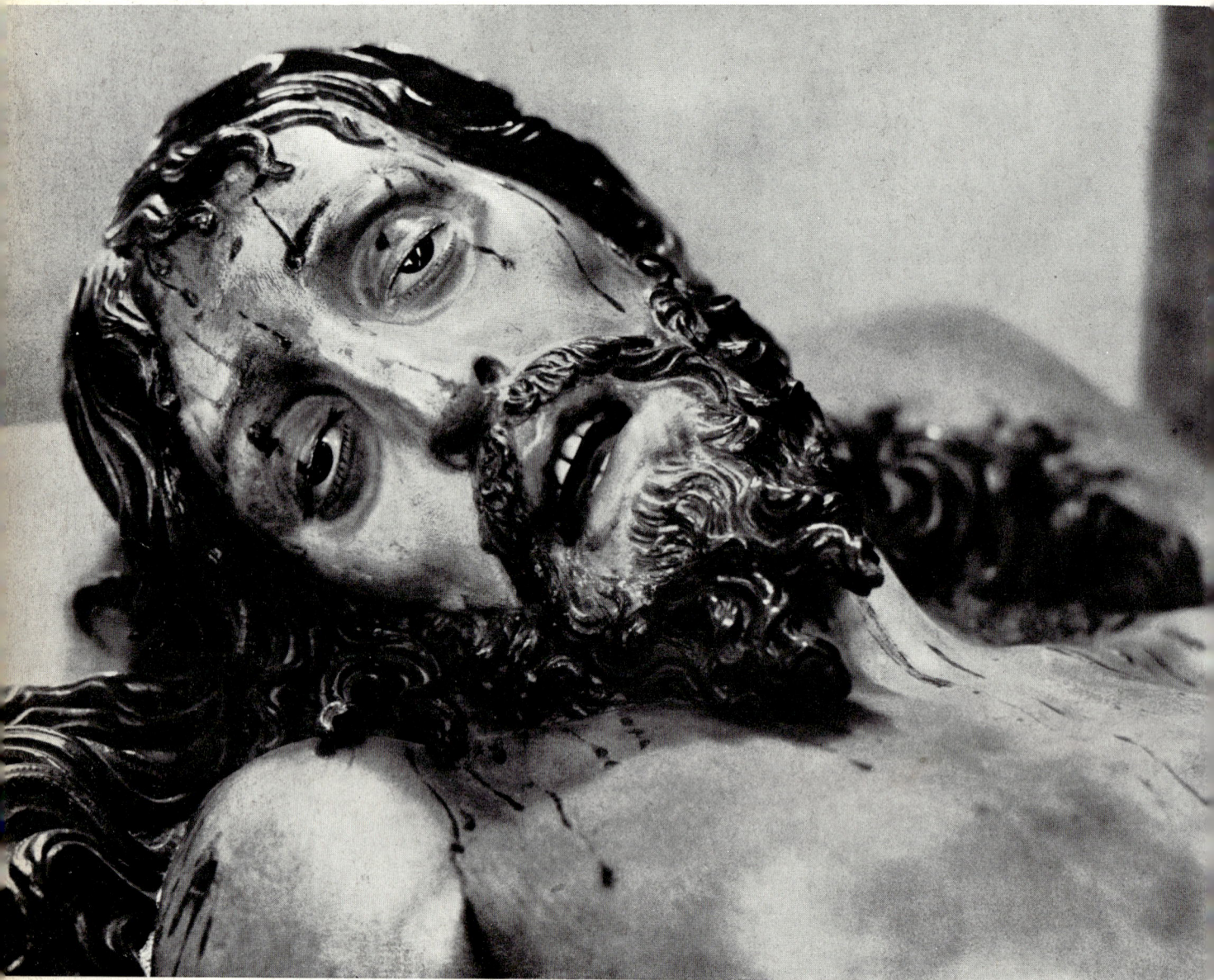

Der theatralische Naturalismus der spanischen Kunst bei Gregorio Fernández läßt den Betrachter die Passion Christi in qualvoller Nähe miterleben.
Valladolid. Museo Nacional de Escultura. Oben: Kopf eines liegenden Christus. 1617. Rechts: Pietà. 1617.

The dramatic realism of the art of Gregorio Fernández brings the beholder into close proximity to Christ's Passion. *Valladolid.* Museo Nacional de Escultura.
Above: head of a recumbent Christ. 1617. Right: Pietà. 1617.

Hessler

Auch in religiösen Werken überwiegt
eine irdische Freude an der menschlichen
Gestalt.
Links: *Rom. S. Andrea della Valle.*
Maria Magdalena. 1606, von Cristoforo
Stati.
Rechts: *Stadthagen bei Hannover.*
Stadtkirche. Mausoleum des Grafen
Ernst von Schaumburg. Nach 1615, von
Adriaen de Vries.

The delight in the human form
predominates even in religious art.
Left: *Rome. S. Andrea della Valle.*
Mary Magdalen. 1606, by Cristoforo
Stati.
Right: *Stadthagen near Hanover.*
Mausoleum of Count Ernst von
Schaumburg. Post 1615,
by Adriaen de Vries.

Alinari

Neumeister

Der Bronzegießer Adriaen de Vries modelliert seine Gruppen kraftvoll mit weit ausgreifenden Konturen.
Links: *Bückeburg*. Stadtkirche. Trägerfiguren vom Taufbecken. 1613—15.
Rechts: *Prag*. Garten des Palais Waldstein. Kampf mit frauenraubendem Kentaur. 1624—26.

Adriaen de Vries' sculptures in bronze are vigorously modelled and of expansive outline.
Left: *Bückeburg*. Parish church. Supporting figures from the font. 1613—15.
Right: *Prague*. Garden of the Waldstein palace. Battle with a centaur. 1624—26.

Busch

In den reformierten Ländern macht der repräsentative Stil der Grabmäler einer privaten Auffassung Platz. Der Tote wird oft mit gelösten Gliedern wie ein Schlafender dargestellt. Oben: *Hatfield, Hertfordshire*. Kirche. Grabmal Sir William Curle. 1612, von Nicholas Stone d. Ä.
Rechts: *Delft*. Nieuwe Kerk. Vom Grabmal Wilhelms des Schweigers: der Verstorbene. 1614–44, von Hendrik de Keyser.

In Protestant countries, the emphasis in tomb art is on the personal rather than the representational aspect. The deceased is frequently shown with relaxed limbs, as if asleep. Above: *Hatfield, Herts*. Parish Church. Tomb of Sir William Curle. 1612, by Nicholas Stone the elder.
Right: *Delft*. Nieuwe Kerk. Tomb of William the Silent. 1614–44, by Hendrik de Keyser.

52

In der handwerklichen Brillanz der Bronzebildwerke von Hans Krumper klingt die große Tradition aus, die das Maximiliansgrab in Innsbruck
hundert Jahre vorher begründet hatte. *München.* Frauenkirche. Zwei Assistenzfiguren vom Grabmal Kaiser Ludwigs d. Bayern.
1619–22. Oben: Detail. Rechts: Herzog Wilhelm IV.

The superb craftsmanship of the bronze sculptures of Hans Krumper is the last reflection of the great tradition begun a century
earlier with the Maximilian tomb in Innsbruck. *Munich.* Frauenkirche. Two figures from the tomb of the Emperor Ludwig the Bavarian.
1619–22. Above: detail. Right: Duke Wilhelm IV.

54

Lauterwasser

Fast unmerklich vollzieht sich
der Wandel vom spätgotischen
Schrein zum barocken Hochaltar.
Links: *Überlingen.*
Stadtpfarrkirche. Hochaltar.
Lindenholz, ungefaßt. 1613–16,
von Jörg Zürn.
Rechts: *Gurk, Kärnten.* Dom.
Hochaltar. Ausschnitt. Holz in
Goldfassung. 1626–32,
von Michael Hönel.

The transition from the Late
Gothic shrine to the Baroque
High Altar takes place almost
unnoticeably.
Left: *Überlingen.* Parish church.
High Altar. Lime wood.
1613–16, by Jörg Zürn.
Right: *Gurk, Carinthia.*
Cathedral. High Altar (detail).
Gilt wood. 1626–32,
by Michael Hönel.

Hessler

Überlingen. Kopf der Maria aus der Verkündigung am Hochaltar (s. S. 56).

Überlingen. Head of the Virgin, from the Annunciation on the High Altar (q. v. ill. 56).

Lauterwasser-Bavaria

Überlingen. Kopf des Erzengels Michael vom Hochaltar (s. S. 56).
Überlingen. Head of St. Michael, from the High Altar (q. v. ill. 56).

Innigkeit in renaissancehaft stillen Formen. *Santiponce bei Sevilla.*
Kloster San Isidoro del Campo. Anbetung der Könige. Relief von einer Altarwand.
1610–12, von Martinez Montañez.

Calm and serenity, reminiscent of the Renaissance. *Santiponce near Seville.*
Convent of San Isidoro del Campo. Adoration of the Kings. Relief from a wall
altar. 1610–12, by Martinez Montañez.

Die Formensprache des Barock kündigt sich an in kraftvoll drängender
Eigenbewegung von Körper und Gewand. *Regensburg.* Niedermünster.
Magdalena unter dem Kreuz. Bronze. Um 1625, wahrscheinlich von Georg Petel.

The vigorous movement of body and draperies already belongs to the formal
language of the Baroque. *Regensburg.* Niedermünster. Mary Magdalen
at the Cross. Bronze. C. 1625, probably by Georg Petel.

Pompöser, vielfach leerer, oft rührender Realismus in der Fülle der Denkmalskunst dieser Zeit. *Magny-en-Vexin, Seine-et-Oise.*
Kirche. Grabmal des Herzogs von Villeroy. 17. Jh.

Realism, sometimes empty and ostentatious, sometimes deeply moving, is characteristic of the tomb art of the time.
Magny-en-Vexin, Seine-et-Oise. Parish church. Tomb of the Duke of Villeroy. 17th cent.

Auch die Anatomie der Wappentiere erhält den Anschein naturgetreuer Wiedergabe. *Elmley Castle, Worcestershire.* Kirche. Grabmal Savage. 1631.

Even the anatomy of armorial beasts is faithfully reproduced from nature. *Elmley Castle, Worcs.* Church. Savage tomb. 1631.

Das spätmittelalterliche Thema des
Totentanzes in einer polnischen
Fassung. *Tartow, Wojewodschaft
Kieleckie.* Jesuskapelle. Tod und
Edelmann. Stuckflachrelief.
1. Hälfte 17. Jh.

The Late Medieval theme of the
Dance of Death in a Polish version.
Tartov, Kieleckie. Jesus chapel.
Death and the nobleman. Stucco bas
relief. First half 17th cent.

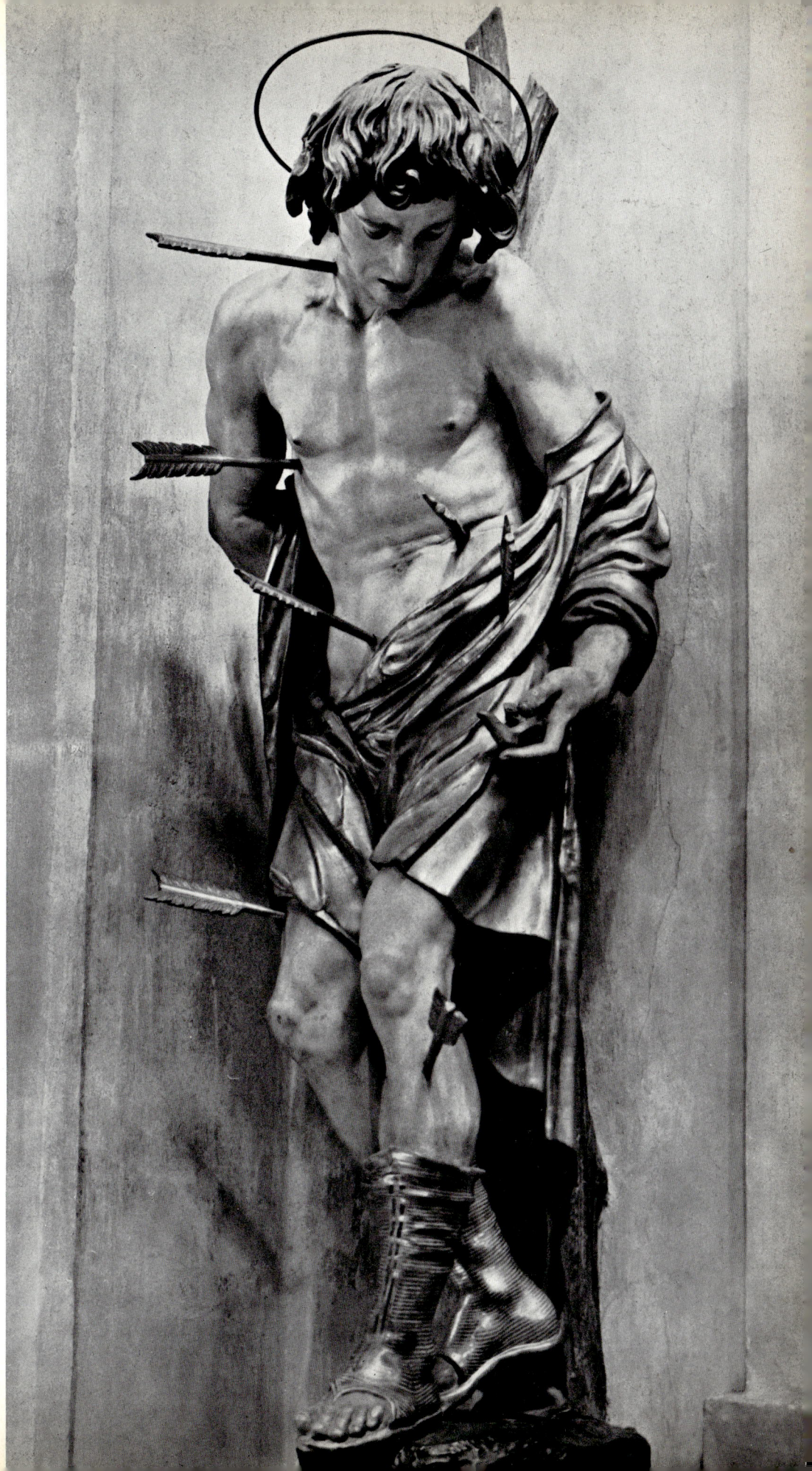

Der nach lebendem Modell studierte
Körper des Heiligen in der Geste des
Zusammenbrechens. *Augsburg.*
St. Moritz. Heiliger Sebastian. Holz.
Um 1627, von Hans Leonhard Gemelich.

The collapsing body of the Saint,
based on the study of a living model.
Augsburg. St. Moritz. St. Sebastian.
Wood. C. 1627,
by Hans Leonhard Gemelich.

Links: Eines der ersten
großen Werke des deutschen
Barock, unmittelbar nach
dem Dreißigjährigen Kriege
entstanden. Maria unter
dem Kreuz, verhalten ihren
Schmerz verbergend.
Bamberg. Dom. Peterschor.
1648–53, von Justus
Gleskher. Holz mit
Goldfassung.

Left: One of the earliest
major works of the German
Baroque, created shortly
after the end of the
Thirty Years' War.
Mary at the foot of the
Cross, her sorrow borne
with restraint. *Bamberg.*
Cathedral. St. Peter's choir.
1648–53, by Justus Gleskher.

Rechts: Veronika mit dem
Schweißtuch Christi,
südländisch-heftig ihren
Schmerz zur Schau stellend.
Rom. St. Peter. Vollendet
1640, von Francesco Mochi.
Marmor.

Right: St. Veronica with the
Holy Kerchief. A southern
figure, freely surrendering
to grief. *Rome.* St. Peter's.
The marble figure was
completed in 1640,
by Francesco Mochi.

Busch   **66**

SANCTA
VERONICA
IEROSOLYMITANA

Gabinetto Fotografico Nazionale

Den Beginn der hochbarocken
Plastik bilden die
Figurengruppen des
zwanzigjährigen Gian Lorenzo
Bernini. Vollkommenes
Vertrautsein mit dem
bewegten menschlichen Körper,
höchste Virtuosität in der
Beherrschung des Marmors.
Links: *London*. Victoria and
Albert Museum. Neptun und
Triton. Um 1620.
Rechts: *Rom*. Galleria Borghese.
Apollo und Daphne. 1622–25.

The figure groups of the
twenty year-old Gian Lorenzo
Bernini form the beginning
of High Baroque sculpture. They
are examples of a complete
mastery of the human body
in movement and of the utmost
virtuosity in the handling of
marble.
Left: *London*. Victoria and
Albert Museum. Neptune and
Triton. C. 1620.
Right: *Rome*. Galleria Borghese.
Apollo and Daphne. 1622–25.

Victoria and Albert Museum **68**

Rom. St. Peter. G. L. Bernini: Konstantin d. Gr. erlebt die Vision des Kreuzes. 1654 bestellt, 1668 vollendet, 1670 aufgestellt.

Rome. St. Peter's. Constantine the Great experiences the Vision of the Cross. By G. L. Bernini. Commissioned in 1654, completed in 1668, placed in its final position in 1670.

Religiöse Ekstase, von Bernini als irdisch-sinnenhaftes Erlebnis faßbar gemacht. *Rom.* Santa Maria della Vittoria.
Die Verzückung der heiligen Theresia von Avila. 1646. (Siehe Farbbild gegenüber Innentitel.)

Religious ecstasy, portrayed by Bernini as sensual experience. *Rome.* Santa Maria della Vittoria. The ecstasy of St. Theresa of Avila.
1646 (q. v. col. frontispice).

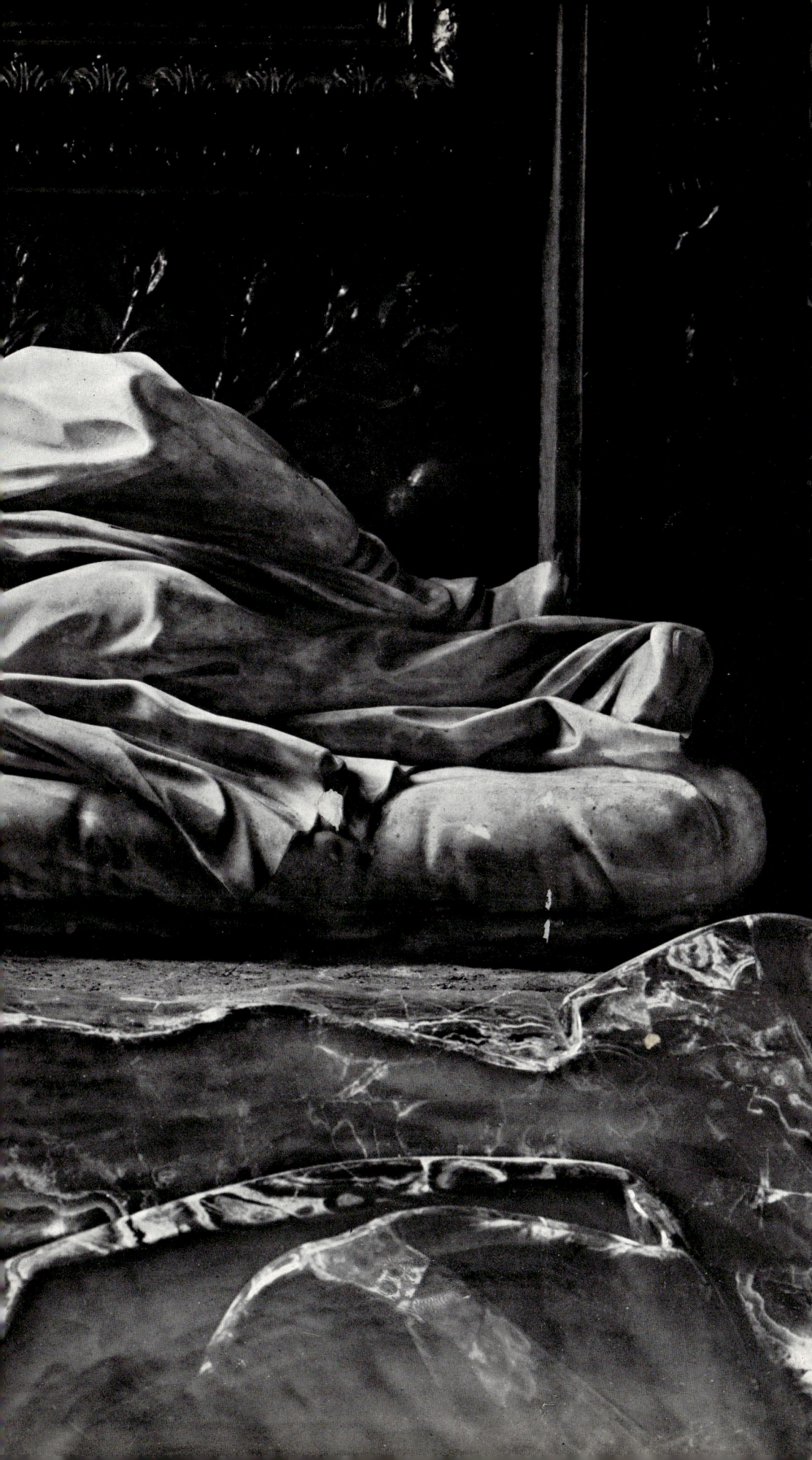

Gabinetto Fotografico Nazionale

Rom. S. Francesco a Ripa.
Der Tod der seligen
Lodovica Albertoni. 1676, von
G. L. Bernini.

Rome. S. Francesco a Ripa.
Death of the Blessed
Lodovica Albertoni. 1676, by
G. L. Bernini.

73

Berninis Meißel läßt die ganze Skala menschlicher Gefühle und Charaktere aus dem Marmor sprechen. Oben: Kopf des Engels aus der Vision der heiligen Theresia von Avila. (Siehe S. 71.) Rechts: *Rom*. Galleria Borghese. Kopf der Statue des David. 1619.

Bernini's chisel evokes the whole range of human emotion and expression. Above: head of the angel, from the vision of St. Theresa of Avila (q. v. ill. 71). Right: *Rome*. Galleria Borghese. Head of David. 1619.

Rom. S. Andrea delle Fratte. Engel mit Dornenkrone, ursprünglich für die Engelsbrücke gearbeitet. 1668, von G. L. Bernini.

Rome. S. Andrea delle Fratte. Angel with the Crown of Thorns, made originally for the Angels' Bridge. 1668, by G. L. Bernini.

Rom. Piazza Navona. Von Berninis Vier-Flüsse-Brunnen: Der Ganges. 1647—52, von Claudio Adam nach dem Entwurf Berninis.

Rome. Piazza Navona. From Bernini's Four River Fountain: the Ganges. 1647—52, by Claudio Adam after Bernini's design.

Rom. Galleria Doria Pamphili. Bildnisbüste der „Papessa" Donna Olimpia Pamphili-Maidalchini. Um 1645, von Alessandro Algardi, neben Bernini der bedeutendste römische Bildhauer des Hochbarock.

Rome. Galleria Doria Pamphili. Portrait bust of the "Papessa" Donna Olimpia Pamphili-Maidalchini. C. 1645, by Alessandro Algardi, next to Bernini one of the most outstanding Roman sculptors of the High Baroque.

von Matt

Rom. S. Lorenzo in Lucina. Bildnisbüste des Arztes Gabriele Fonseca. 1665—68, von Gian Lorenzo Bernini. Einer der Höhepunkte barocker Porträtplastik.

Rome. S. Lorenzo in Lucina. Portrait bust of the physician Gabriele Fonseca. 1665—68, by Gian Lorenzo Bernini. One of the greatest triumphs of Baroque portrait sculpture.

Foto Marburg

Alinari

Charakteristische Beispiele der Gruppierung plastischer Werke, entworfen als Teile eines architektonischen Gesamtkunstwerkes.
Oben: *Rom*. Kirche Gesù e Maria. Grabmal Pietro und Francesco di Bolognetti. Vor 1675, von Francesco Cavallini. Rechts: *Rom*. Kirche Il Gesù. Figuren in der Fensterzone. 1668–83, von Antonio Raggi.

Characteristic examples of groupings, designed as parts of an architectural ensemble. Above: *Rome*. Church of Gesù e Maria. Tomb of Pietro and Francesco di Bolognetti. Pre 1675, by Francesco Cavallini. Right: *Rome*. Church of Il Gesù. Figures in the window zone. 1668–83, by Antonio Raggi.

In der Nachfolge Berninis gewinnt das Relief die kompositorische Geschmeidigkeit der Malerei. *Rom. S. Agnese in Piazza Navona. Linker Seitenaltar:* Tod der hl. Cäcilia. Ausschnitt. Um 1670–80, von Antonio Raggi.

Among Bernini's successors, the relief attains a facility of composition hitherto confined to painting. *Rome. S. Agnese in Piazza Navona.* Left altar: death of St. Cecilia. Detail, c. 1670–80, by Antonio Raggi.

von Matt

83   *Rom.* S. Agnese in Piazza Navona. Rechter Seitenaltar: Steinigung der hl. Emerentiana. Ausschnitt. Um 1670–80, von Ercole Ferrata.
Rome. S. Agnese in Piazza Navona. Right altar: the Stoning of St. Emerentiana. Detail, c. 1670–80, by Ercole Ferrata.

Hochbarock in der deutschen Schnitzkunst. Links: *St. Georgen a. d. Mattig, Oberösterreich*. Vom Altar der Filialkirche: Tod des hl. Sebastian. Um 1650—55, von Martin und Michael Zürn d. Ä. Oben: *Preetz, Holstein*. Ehem. Klosterkirche. Vom Fragment eines Altars aus Dänischhagen: Anbetende an der Krippe. 1656, von Hans Gudewerth d. J.

German wood sculpture in the High Baroque. Left: *St. Georgen a. d. Mattig, Upper Austria*. From the altar of the Filialkirche: Death of St. Sebastian. C. 1650—55, by Martin and Michael Zürn the elder. Above: *Preetz, Holstein*. Former convent church. Worshippers at the crib. Detail, from the fragment of an altar formerly at Dänischhagen. 1656, by Hans Gudewerth the younger.

Schildknecht

Schleswig. Dom. Portal zur Gruft der Familie Eilhard Schacht.
1670, von einem unbekannten Meister.

Schleswig. Cathedral. Entrance to the tomb of the Eilhard Schacht family.
1670, by an unknown master.

Brüssel. Stiftskirche St. Michael und St. Gudula. Engel der Erleuchtung an einem
Beichtstuhl. 17. Jh., von einem unbekannten Meister.

Brussels. Convent church of St. Michael and St. Gudula. Angel,
from a confessional. 17th cent., by an unknown master.

MAS

MAS

Andachtsbilder des Barock in Spanien. Links: *Madrid*. Academia S. Fernando.
Heiliger Bruno. 1650–60, von Manuel Pereyra. Rechts: *Toledo*. Kathedrale. Capilla S. Pedro. Franz von Assisi. Um 1675, von Pedro de Mena.

Devotional figures of the Baroque in Spain. Left: *Madrid*. Academia S. Fernando. St. Bruno. 1650–60, by Manuel Pereyra. Right: *Toledo*. Cathedral.
Capilla S. Pedro. St. Francis of Assisi. C. 1675, by Pedro de Mena.

Granada. Kathedrale. Sakristei.
La Virgen (die Jungfrau Maria).
1656, von Alonso Cano.

Granada. Cathedral. Sacristy.
La Virgen.
1656, by Alonso Cano.

MAS

Verherrlichung des Gottherrschers im absolutistischen Frankreich. *Versailles*. Schloß. Wanddekoration im „Salon de la Guerre". Ludwig XIV. zu Pferde. Stuck. Um 1680, von Antoine Coyzevox.

The deification of the monarch in absolutist France. *Versailles*. Wall decoration in the "Salon de la Guerre". Louis XIV on horseback. C. 1680, by Antoine Coyzevox.

Die Taten des Herrschers, als Zeitreportage im
Relief festgehalten. *Paris*. Louvre.
Rechts: Eroberung von Valenciennes. 1686, von
Jean Arnould und Pierre le Nègre. Unten:
Übergang über den Rhein. 1680—86,
von Martin van den Bogaert, genannt Desjardins.

Scenes from the life of the ruler, portrayed in
contemporary reliefs. *Paris*. Louvre.
Right: the capture of Valenciennes. 1686,
by Jean Arnould and Pierre le Nègre.
Below: crossing the Rhine. 1680—86,
by Martin van den Bogaert, called Desjardins.

Versailles. Grotten im Schloßpark. Antike Szenen als allegorische Huldigung an Ludwig XIV. Oben: Apollo und Nymphen. 1666–75, von François Girardon. Rechts: Tränken der Rosse des Helios. Nach 1667, von Gilles Guérin.

Versailles. Grottos in the park. Classic scenes as allegoric homage to Louis XIV. Above: Apollo and nymphs. 1666–75, by François Girardon. Right: watering the horses of Helios. Post 1667, by Gilles Guérin.

Kersting

Unzählige Bildnisbüsten und Grabmäler zeugen, zumal in Frankreich, vom Repräsentationsverlangen der Zeit. Oben: *Paris*. Louvre. Der Dichter Nicolas Boileau-Despréaux. Um 1690, von François Girardon. Rechts: *Paris*. St. Eustache. Grabmal Colberts, des Ministers Ludwigs XIV. 1685—87, von Antoine Coyzevox.

Innumerable portrait busts and tombs are evidence of the longing for ostentation, particularly in France. Above: *Paris*. Louvre.
The poet Nicolas Boileau-Despréaux. C. 1690, by François Girardon. Right: *Paris*. St. Eustache. Tomb of Colbert, chief minister of Louis XIV. 1685—87, by Antoine Coyzevox.

94

QVÆ SVRSVM SV
NON QVÆ SVPE

Paris. Louvre. Der Minister Kardinal Mazarin, von seinem Grabmal. 1692, von Antoine Coyzevox. Rechts: Grabmal des Herzogs Charles de la Vieuville   Foto Marburg
(gest. 1653), aus der einstigen Kirche Des Minimes in Paris. Von Gilles Guérin.

Paris. Louvre. Cardinal Mazarin, from his tomb. 1692, by Antoine Coyzevox. Right: tomb of Duke Charles de la Vieuville (d. 1653), from the former Eglise
des Minimes in Paris. By Gilles Guérin.

This Monument was designed to be Erect
before the decease of S[r] John Richard[?]
Earl of Dorset, Father of this Noble
who departed this life 27th of August
in the year of our Lord God 1677
And in the 58 year of his age And [?]
By Hen[?] ... ... Dowager of
Dorset ... ...
And ... ... Memory
Erected ... ...
of her in ... ... rever
our ... ...

Trauernde Gestalten umgeben den Sarkophag mit dem Abbild des Verstorbenen. Links: *Withyam Church, Sussex.* Grabmal Sackville.
1677, von Caius Gabriel Cibber. Oben: *Paris.* Kapelle der Sorbonne. Grabmal Richelieus. 1694, von François Girardon.

Mourning figures surround the sarcophagus with the portrait of the deceased. Left: *Withyam Church, Sussex.* Tomb of the Sackville family.
1677, by Caius Gabriel Cibber. Above: *Paris.* Chapel of the Sorbonne. Tomb of Richelieu. 1694, by François Girardon.

Foto Marburg

Traubenkraut

Gent. S. Bavo. Grabmal des Bischofs Antoine Triest. Gestorben 1657. Von Jérome Duquesnoy. Ausschnitt.

Ghent. S. Bavo. Tomb of Bishop Antoine Triest (detail). D. 1657. By Jérome Duquesnoy.

Trier. Liebfrauenkirche. Grabmal des Domherrn Karl von Metternich. Um 1675, von Matthias Rauchmiller. Ausschnitt.

Trier. Liebfrauenkirche. Tomb of Canon Karl von Metternich (detail). C. 1675, by Matthias Rauchmiller.

100

Foto Marburg

Wilde Kraft und dynamische Bewegung
kennzeichnen das Werk von
Pierre Puget (1620—94) — eine
Ausnahmeerscheinung im vorwiegend
klassisch repräsentierenden Barock
Frankreichs.
Links: *Paris*. Louvre. „Hercule gaulois",
Tonskizze zu einer Marmorskulptur.
Um 1660.
Rechts: *Genua*. S. Maria de Carignano.
Heiliger Sebastian. 1661—65.

Strength and dynamism are
characteristic of the work of Pierre Puget
(1620—94) — an exception in the
predominantly Classic and
representational Baroque art of France.
Left: *Paris*. Louvre. "Hercule gaulois,"
clay study for a marble figure. C. 1660.
Right: *Genoa*. S. Maria de Carignano.
St. Sebastian. 1661—65.

Giraudon **102**

Foto Marburg

Links: *Paris*. Louvre (früher im Park
von Versailles). Perseus befreit
Andromeda. Vollendet 1684,
von Pierre Puget.
Rechts: *Paris*. Louvre. Alexander als
Sieger. Vor 1668, von Pierre Puget.

Left: *Paris*. Louvre (formerly in the park
of Versailles). Perseus and
Andromeda. C. 1684, by Pierre Puget.
Right: *Paris*. Louvre. The victorious
Alexander. Pre 1668, by Pierre Puget.

Lieblingsgeschöpfe des Barock:
Jugendliche Engel von beschwingter Schönheit.
Lüttich. Museum Curtius. Tonskizze. 1681,
von Jean Delcour.

Favourite figures of the Baroque:
youthful angels of grace and beauty.
Liège, Belgium. Museum Curtius. Clay study. 1681,
by Jean Delcour.

106

Michael Zürn d. J. schuf Engel,
die in ihrem tänzerischen Schwung
süddeutsche Gegenstücke zu Berninis
Gestalten sind (vgl. S. 76).
Kremsmünster, Oberösterreich,
Stiftskirche. Marmor. 1683.

Michael Zürn the younger created
angels who, in their graceful movement,
are like German counterparts to
Bernini's figures (q. v. ill. 76).
Kremsmünster, Upper Austria. Convent
Church. 1683.

Alinari

Foto Marburg

Gent. S. Bavo. An Michelangelo und Raffael erinnern Anmut und Stille der Madonna vom Grabmal d'Allamont. Nach 1670, von Jean Delcour.

Ghent. S. Bavo. In her grace and calm the Madonna from the d'Allamont tomb recalls Raphael and Michelangelo. Post 1670, by Jean Delcour.

Florenz. SS. Annunziata. Cappella Francesco Feroni. Engel in den Zwickeln unter der Vierungskuppel. 1692, von Giovanni Battista Foggini.

Florence. SS. Annunziata. Cappella Francesco Feroni. Angels in the spandrels of the dome above the crossing. 1692, by Giovanni Battista Foggini.

Ehm

Prag. Kreuzherrenkirche. Zwei Werke (1689–90) des vorwiegend in Böhmen tätigen Max Conrad Süssner. Links: Der hl. Johann Nepomuk.
Oben: Der hl. Martin.
Prague. Kreuzherrenkirche. Two works (1689–90) of Max Conrad Süssner, a master chiefly active in Bohemia. Left: St. John Nepomuk. Above: St. Martin.

Hessler

Im österreichischen Hochbarock wird volkstümliche Innigkeit veredelt durch festlichen Glanz. Links: *St. Wolfgang, Salzkammergut*. Marienkrönung vom Doppelaltar. 1675–76, von Thomas Schwanthaler. Oben: *Lochen, Oberösterreich*. Maria mit Kind aus dem Hochaltar. 1709–13, von Meinrad Guggenbichler.

In the Austrian High Baroque, festive splendour mingles with a simple piety. Left: *St. Wolfgang, Salzkammergut*. The Coronation of the Virgin, from the winged altar. 1675–76, by Thomas Schwanthaler. Above: *Lochen, Upper Austria*. Virgin and Child, from the High Altar. 1709–13, by Meinrad Guggenbichler.

113

Decker

Schmerz des Martyriums im Übergang zur Verklärung. *Schleedorf bei Salzburg.*
Kopf des sterbenden Stephanus von der zerstörten Mittelgruppe am ehemaligen Hochaltar. 1701, von Meinrad Guggenbichler.

The anguish of martyrdom in the transition to ecstasy. *Schleedorf near Salzburg.* Head of the dying St. Stephen from the centre group
(now destroyed) of the former High Altar. 1701, by Meinrad Guggenbichler.

Carvajal

Valladolid. Museo Nacional de Escultura. Kopf des hl. Paulus. 1707, von Juan Alonso Villabrille y Ron.

Valladolid. Museo Nacional de Escultura. Head of St. Paul. 1707, by Juan Alonso Villabrille y Ron.

Links: *Prag*. Karlskirche. Heilige Treppe.
Christus an der Martersäule. Farbig gefaßte
Holzplastik. 1720—40, von
Jan Jirí Slanzovsky.
Rechts: *Wien*. Kapuzinerkirche. Maria vom
Gruftaltar der rechten Kapelle. 1711—17,
von Peter von Strudel.

Left: *Prague*. Church of St. Charles.
Calvary steps. Christ at the pillar. Painted
wood sculpture. 1720—40, by
Jan Jirí Slanzovsky.
Right: *Vienna*. Kapuzinerkirche.
The Virgin, from the sepulchral altar in the
right chapel. 1711—17,
by Peter von Strudel.

Die Karlsbrücke in *Prag* ist außerhalb Italiens das berühmteste Beispiel der mit plastischen Andachtsbildern geschmückten Brücken, die jetzt überall in Europa entstehen. Rechts: Madonna mit den Heiligen Thomas von Aquino und Dominikus. 1708, von Matthäus Wenzel Jäckel.

The 'Charles bridge in *Prague* is, outside of Italy, the most famous example of a bridge decorated with devotional sculpture. Right: Madonna with St. Thomas of Aquino and St. Dominic. 1708, by Matthäus Wenzel Jäckel.

Die Gegenreformation läßt allenthalben Heiligensäulen und Andachtsbilder entstehen. Oben: *Wien*. Pestsäule am Graben.
1687, von Benkert, Strudel und Rauchmiller nach Entwurf des Architekten Fischer von Erlach. Ausschnitt.
Rechts: *Bamberg*. Am Alten Ebracher Hof. Vision des hl. Bernhard. 1623—24, von Johann Eberhard Goldwitzer.

Figures of Saints and devotional groups appear everywhere in the wake of the Counter Reformation. Above: *Vienna*. The Plague column
on the Graben. 1687, by Benkert, Strudel and Rauchmiller, after the design of Fischer von Erlach. Detail.
Right: *Bamberg*. From the "Alter Ebracher Hof." Vision of St. Bernard. 1623—24, by Johann Eberhard Goldwitzer.

Bauer

120

Hessler

Gestalten des Alltags werden darstellenswert. Oben: *St. Pölten bei Wien.* Schweighof. Landmann mit Garben. Nach 1696, von einem unbekannten Meister.
Rechts: *Salzburg.* Hofmarstallschwemme. Roßknecht. 1695, von Bernhard Michael Mandl. 1732 verändert aufgestellt.

Figures from everyday life are increasingly shown in art. Above: *St. Pölten near Vienna.* Schweighof. Reaping peasant. Post 1696, by an unknown master.
Right: *Salzburg.* Fountain of the former imperial stables. A groom. 1695, by Bernhard Michael Mandl. Placed in its present position 1732, after some alterations.

PVLChrItVDo ANTIQVA
MIrabILI noVItate
restITVta.
A
Celsissimo, AC Reverendissimo
DOMINO DOMINO
LEOPOLDO
ANTONIO ELEUTHERIO,
ARCHIEPISCOPO,
et Saci Rom: Imp:
PRINCIPE SALISBURGENSI,
Sac Sedis Apostolicæ Legato Nato,
Germaniæ Primate,
ET ANTIQUISS: LIBERIS BARONIBUS
DE FIRMIAN & C. & C.

Andreas Schlüter ist die überragende Künstlergestalt des deutschen Hochbarock. Oben: *Homburg v. d. H.* Schloß. Landgraf Friedrich II.,
brandenburgischer General, Kleists „Prinz von Homburg". 1704. Rechts: *Berlin.* Schloß Charlottenburg. Der Große Kurfürst,
Friedrich Wilhelm I. von Brandenburg. 1698–1709. Ehemals Schloßbrücke.

Andreas Schlüter is the most outstanding master of the German High Baroque. Above: *Homburg v. d. H.* Castle. Landgrave Friedrich II,
the "Prinz von Homburg." 1704. Right: *Berlin.* Schloss Charlottenburg. Monument of Friedrich Wilhelm I of Brandenburg. 1698–1709.

Berlin. Domgruft. Der Tod am Sarkophag der Königin Sophie Charlotte, Gemahlin Friedrichs I. 1705, von Andreas Schlüter.

Berlin. Cathedral tombs. Death, from the sarcophagus of Queen Sophie Charlotte, consort of Friedrich I. 1705, by Andreas Schlüter.

Berlin. Rittersaal des 1950 abgerissenen Schlosses. Wanddekoration: Gruppe „Europa". Um 1700, von Andreas Schlüter.

Berlin. Rittersaal (Knights' chamber) of the former palace (demolished in 1950). "Europa" group. C. 1700, by Andreas Schlüter.

126

Oertel-Film

Erschütternde Kraft des
Ausdrucks in Schlüters Masken
sterbender Krieger.
Berlin. Zeughaus. Zwei der
einundzwanzig
Fensterschlußsteine im Innenhof.
Sandstein. Um 1698.

Schlüter's masks of dying
warriors almost overwhelm
in the intensity of their
expressions.
Berlin. Zeughaus. Two of
twenty-one keystones from the
windows in the inner courtyard.
Sandstone. C. 1698.

Neumeister   128

Rußland erfährt durch Peter den Großen den vollen Einfluß europäischer Kunst.
Leningrad. Peter-Pauls-Dom. Bilderwand. Nach 1703, von einem unbekannten westlichen Meister. Dombau von Domenico Tressini.

Through Peter the Great, Russia experiences the full impact of European art. *Leningrad.* Cathedral of SS. Peter and Paul. Iconostasis. Post 1703, by an unknown Western master.

130

Mainz. Dom. Grabmal für den Dompropst Heinrich Ferdinand von der Leyen. Gestorben 1714. Wahrscheinlich von Johann Mauritz Gröninger.

Mainz. Cathedral. Tomb of Dean Heinrich Ferdinand von der Leyen. D. 1714. Probably by Johann Mauritz Gröninger.

131

Decker

Fischbach im Taunus. Pfarrkirche. Immaculata aus Schloßborn.
Um 1735, von einem unbekannten Meister.

Fischbach, Taunus. Parish church. Immaculata from Schlossborn.
C. 1735, by an unknown master.

Wien. Akademie der bildenden Künste. Engel vom ehemaligen Hochaltar
der Stiftskirche Heiligenkreuz, Niederösterreich. 1699, von Giovanni Giuliani.

Vienna. Akademie der bildenden Künste. Angel from the former High Altar
of the convent church at Heiligenkreuz, Lower Austria. 1699, by Giovanni Giuliani.

Auf dem Wege zum Rokoko:
Manieristische Züge leben wieder
auf. *Palermo*. Oratorio del Rosario.
Eine der Tugenden: Fortitudo. Stuck.
1714–17, von Giacomo Serpotta.

At the threshold of the Rococo:
Mannerist features come to life
again. *Palermo*. Oratorio del
Rosario. One of the virtues.
Fortitudo. 1714–17,
by Giacomo Serpotta.

Römische Kunst, stets kraftvoll
im Ausdruck, sprengt den
architektonischen Rahmen. *Rom*.
S. Giovanni in Laterano.
Heiliger Matthäus. 1713–15,
von Camillo Rusconi.

Roman art, always of vigorous
expression, bursts through the
architectural frame. *Rome*.
S. Giovanni in Laterano. St. Matthew.
1713–15, by Camillo Rusconi.

London. Victoria and Albert Museum. Samson und dér Löwe. Terrakotta. 1706, von Michael van der Voort.
London. Victoria and Albert Museum. Samson and the lion. Terracotta. 1706, by Michael van der Voort.

Neumeister

Prag. Klemenskirche. Maria Magdalena von einem Beichtstuhl. Holz. 1715—21, von Matthias Bernhard Braun aus Ötz in Tirol.

Prague. Church of St. Clement. Mary Magdalena, from a confessional. 1715—21, by Matthias Bernhard Braun.

Ehm

Gebilde weltflüchtiger, natursuchender Phantasie bevölkern manche Parkanlage des Spätbarock. *Bethlehemwald bei Kuks in Böhmen*. Der Eremit Garinus. 1729, von Matthias Bernhard Braun.

Forms inspired by an enthusiasm for nature form a feature of many Late Baroque parks. *Bethlehemwald near Kuks, Bohemia*. The hermite Garinus. 1729, by Matthias Bernhard Braun.

Im Primitiven sucht eine überfeinerte Welt das Natürliche zu fassen. *Wien.* Schwarzenberg-Palais. Zerlumpte Alte mit Schwein. 1712–38, von Lorenzo Mattielli.

A highly sophisticated age seeks nature through the image of roughness and simplicity. *Vienna.* Schwarzenberg palace. Ragged old woman with a pig. 1712–38, by Lorenzo Mattielli.

139

Edwin Smith

Roubier

Beyer

Versailles. Park. Kopf des Giganten Enceladus, von einem der
Wasserbecken. Blei. 1746, von Gaspard Marsy.

Versailles. Park. Head of the giant Enceladus, from the fountain of
Apollo. Lead. 1746, by Gaspard Marsy.

Dresden. Zwinger. Karyatiden vom Wallpavillon.
1709, von Balthasar Permoser.

Dresden. Zwinger. Caryatids from the wall pavilion.
1709, by Balthasar Permoser.

Allegorische Verherrlichung
hochstehender Zeitgenossen.
Links: *Valec bei Karlsbad.*
Apotheose des Grafen Sporck.
Nach einem Abguß in der
Nationalgalerie Prag. 1733, aus
der Werkstatt des Matthias
Bernhard Braun.
Rechts: *Wien.* Barockmuseum im
Unteren Belvedere. Apotheose
des Prinzen Eugen. Marmor.
1718–21, von Balthasar Permoser.

Allegoric glorification of great
contemporaries.
Left: *Valec near Karlsbad.*
The apotheosis of Count Sporck.
After a cast in the National
Gallery, Prague. 1733, from the
workshop of Matthias Bernhard
Braun.
Right: *Vienna.* Barockmuseum
im Unteren Belvedere.
Apotheosis of Prince Eugen.
Marble. 1718–21, by
Balthasar Permoser.

Berlin. Staatliche Museen. Herkules.
Um 1720, von Balthasar Permoser.

Berlin. Staatliche Museen. Hercules.
C. 1720, by Balthasar Permoser.

Leipzig. Stadtgeschichtliches Museum. „Die Verdammnis". Marmor.
Nach 1722, von Balthasar Permoser.

Leipzig. Stadtgeschichtliches Museum. "Damnation." Marble.
Post 1722, by Balthasar Permoser.

Gent. S. Bavo. Kanzelfuß: Die Wahrheit zeigt der erwachenden
Menschheit die Heilige Schrift. 1745, von Laurent Delvaux.

Ghent. S. Bavo. Truth shows the Holy Writ to the awakening human
race. From the pulpit base. 1745, by Laurent Delvaux.

146

Novais

Portugiesische Werke aus der ersten Hälfte des 18. Jahrhunderts, von unbekannten Meistern.
Links: *Braga*. Igreja dos Jesuítas. Johannes der Evangelist.
Rechts: *Lissabon*. Nossa Senhora da Pena. Atlanten vom Hochaltar.
Beide Werke aus Holz.

Portuguese wood sculptures of the first half of the eighteenth century, by unknown masters.
Left: *Braga*. Igreja dos Jesuítas. St. John the Evangelist.
Right: *Lisbon*. Nossa Senhora da Pena. Atlantes, from the High Altar.

Wie in der Spätgotik, so ist auch im deutschen Spätbarock die erregte Sprache des Gewandes vielfach ein Gleichnis des Seelischen. *Berlin*. Staatliche Museen. Maria Immaculata, aus *Eigelstetten bei Donauwörth*. Lindenholz. Um 1735, von Hans Georg Bschorer.

In the German Late Baroque, as in the Late Gothic, the agitated language of the draperies is often an expression of inner tension. *Berlin*. Staatliche Museen. Maria Immaculata, from *Eigelstetten near Donauwörth*. Lime wood. C. 1735, by Hans Georg Bschorer.

Metten, Niederbayern. Benediktinerklosterkirche. Heilige Anna vom rechten Seitenaltar. Weißer Glanzstuck. Lebensgroß. 1722—24, von Franz Josef Ignaz Holzinger.

· *Metten, Lower Bavaria*. Church of the Benedictine convent. St. Anne, from the right side altar. White stucco, highly polished. Life size. 1722—24, by Franz Josef Ignaz Holzinger.

Decker

Hege

Neumeister

Der Effekt des „Schwebens" einer Plastik im Raum, von Egid Quirin Asam zu höchster Vollendung gebracht. Links: *Rohr, Niederbayern*. Hochaltar der Klosterkirche. Himmelfahrt Mariens. Stuck. 1723. Oben: *München*. Johann Nepomuk-Kirche, genannt „Asamkirche". Gnadenstuhl über dem Hochaltar. Stuck. Um 1740.

The effect of sculpture floating in space, brought to the highest perfection by Egid Quirin Asam. Left: *Rohr, Lower Bavaria*. High Altar of the convent church. The Ascension. Stucco. 1723. Above: *Munich*. Johann Nepomuk-Kirche, called "Asamkirche." Mercy seat above the High Altar. Stucco. C. 1740.

Der Spätbarock, auch Rokoko genannt, als internationaler Stil höfischer Eleganz. Oben: *London*. Victoria and Albert Museum. Terrakottamodell zum Grabmal des Dr. Hugh Chamberlen. Um 1730, von Peter Scheemaker. Rechts: *Altötting, Oberbayern*. Gnadenkapelle. Kurprinz Maximilian Joseph von Bayern. Silber. 1737, von Wilhelm de Groff.

The late Baroque, also called Rococo, emerges as an international style of courtly elegance. Above: *London*. Victoria and Albert Museum. Terracotta model for the tomb of Dr. Hugh Chamberlen. C. 1730, by Peter Scheemaker. Right: *Altötting, Upper Bavaria*. Mercy chapel. The Elector Maximilian Joseph of Bavaria. Silver. 1737, by Wilhelm de Groff.

G. de Grof. Inu et fec

Roubier

Um die Mitte des 18. Jahrhunderts: Beginn einer „privateren", weniger repräsentativen Darstellungsweise im Bildnis. Links: *London*. Victoria and Albert Museum. Oliver Cromwell. 1762, von Joseph Wilton. Oben: *Paris*. Louvre. Der Bildhauer Nicolas Coustou. Um 1730, von seinem Bruder Guillaume Coustou.

Around the middle of the eighteenth century the representative manner gives way to a more intimate style of portraiture. Left: *London*. Victoria and Albert Museum. Oliver Cromwell. 1762, by Joseph Wilton. Above: *Paris*. Louvre. The sculptor Nicolas Coustou. C. 1730, by his brother Guillaume Coustou.

157

Manieristische Phase des späten Barock: Selbst Tugenden und Heilige werden in fast koketter Geziertheit wiedergegeben. Links: *Rom. S. Giovanni in Laterano. Cappella Orsini. Temperantia. Um 1735, von Filippo della Valle. Oben: *Rom. St. Peter. Der hl. Bruno. 1744, von René Michel Slodtz, genannt Michelange.

The Mannerist phase of the Late Baroque: even Virtues and Saints are now of an almost affected grace. Left: *Rome. S. Giovanni in Laterano. Cappella Orsini. Temperantia. C. 1735, by Filippo della Valle. Above: *Rome. St. Peter's. St. Bruno. 1744, by René Michel Slodtz, called Michelange.

159

Boger

Boger   Diego F. Carlone schuf in Süddeutschland Gestalten im römischen Stil. *Weingarten*. Klosterkirche. Links: Joachim, von einem Querschiffsaltar.
Oben: Engel von einem Seitenaltar. Nach 1720.

In Southern Germany, Diego F. Carlone created figures in the Roman manner. *Weingarten*. Convent church.
Left: St. Joachim, from a transept altar. Above: angel, from a side altar. Post 1720.

Im habsburgischen Reich schafft Georg Raphael Donner Werke von klassischer Kraft und Harmonie. Oben: *Wien*. Barockmuseum. Der Fluß Traun vom Providentia-Brunnen am Neuen Markt. Blei. 1739. Rechts: *Preßburg*. Dom. Der hl. Martin und der Bettler. Vom ehem. Hochaltar. Blei. 1735.

In the Habsburg empire, Georg Raphael Donner's work attains a Classic force and harmony. Above: *Vienna*. Barockmuseum. The river Traun, from the Providentia fountain on the Neuer Markt. Lead. 1739. Right: *Bratislava*. Cathedral. St. Martin and the beggar. From the former High Altar. Lead. 1735.

Decker

Akademie der Wissenschaften Budapest

Aus dem Werk Georg Raphael Donners. Oben: *Gurk, Kärnten*. Dom. Hände aus einer Gruppe der Beweinung Christi. Blei. 1740/41.
Rechts: *Budapest*. National-Museum. Engel vom ehemaligen Hochaltar des Domes in Preßburg. Blei. 1733—35.

Works by Georg Raphael Donner. Above: *Gurk, Carinthia*. Cathedral. Hands, from a group of the Lamentation. Lead. 1740/41.
Right: *Budapest*. National Museum. An angel, from the former High Altar in Bratislava cathedral. Lead. 1733—35.

164

Der französische Barock trägt durchweg klassizistische Züge. *Paris*. Links: Champs Elysées. Rossebändiger aus der Gruppe der sogenannten „Pferde von Marly". 1740–45, von Guillaume Coustou. Oben: Fontaine de Grenelle. 1739–45, von Edme Bouchardon.

Classic traits prevail in French Baroque. *Paris*. Left: Champs Elysées. Horse tamer, from the group of the so-called "Horses of Marly." 1740–45, by Guillaume Coustou. Above: Fontaine de Grenelle. 1739–45, by Edme Bouchardon.

167

Wasserspiele des späten Barock in Italien. Oben: *Caserta bei Neapel.* Diana-Brunnen im Schloßpark. Nach 1752. Rechts: *Rom.* Fontana Trevi. 1762, Mittelgruppe von Pietro Bracci.

Late Baroque fountains in Italy. Above: *Caserta near Naples.* Diana fountain in the palace grounds. Post 1752. Right: *Rome.* Fontana Trevi. 1762, centre group by Pietro Bracci.

168

Verismus im Dienste volkstümlicher Anschaulichkeit. Oben: *Weißenregen, Bayer. Wald.* Wallfahrtskirche. Fischerkanzel. 1785, von Johannes Paulus Hager.
Rechts: *Neapel.* S. Severo. Vom Grabmal Antonio Sangro: Die Befreiung vom Irrtum. Nach 1750, von Francesco Queirolo.

Realism in the service of popular illustration. Above: *Weissenregen, Bavarian Forest.* Pilgrimage church. Fishermen pulpit. 1785, by Johannes Paulus Hager.
Right: *Naples.* S. Severo. From the tomb of Antonio Sangro. The liberation from error. Post 1750, by Francesco Queirolo.

EQVES FRANCISCVS QVEIROLI IANVENSIS FECIT

NAHVM CAP.I.
VERS.XIII.

...GVLA RV...
...ERVMPAM,
VINCVLA
...IBI ARVM...
...T LONGA NOCT...
...VIBVS ME
...CON...INEB...
...A NON QVA...
...M MVNDO
...NERIS

SABBATI AE
CAP.XXII.
VERS.II.

PAVLI AD CORIN...
CAP.XI.
VERS.XXXII.

ANTONIO SANGRIO
...VCI TVRRIS MAIORIS
...AVLI SANSEVERI
PRINCIPIS FILIO
ELOQVENTIA INGENIO
VARIAQ·FORTVNA ADMIRABILI
QVI QVVM VXORE
IN ADOLESCENTIA AMISSA
CAELEBS DEIN
IVVENILIBVS CVPIDITATIBVS
SATIS SVPERO ...APVISSET
PROPTER...AQVE
PATRIA PROCVL ...VROPAM OMNEM
PERAGRA...SET
IDEMQ· CO...NITIS
TANDEM ERRORIBVS
REDVX SACERDOS
HVIVS TEMPLI ABEAS
SANCTITATE PIOR ...ENSIONI
VI·D· SEPT· ...N· MDCCLVII
A...· SVAE LXXII OBIISSET DOCVIT
NON ...ATVI...ISSE
HVMANAE IMBECILLITATI
VT MAGNAE SI...VIRIS VIRTVTES
EX...TANT
RAIMVNDVS SANSEVEPI
...RINCEPS FILIVS
NE QVID ...TI NE QVID VERITATI
DEM...RET
EIVS...OD ELOGIVM
INSCRIBEN...V ...ONEN...VMQVE
...VRA...VIT

Aufsberg

Busch

Architektur, von Plastik gleichsam in schwingende Bewegung versetzt. Links: Wallfahrtskirche *In der Wies bei Steingaden, Oberbayern.*
Blick in den Chor. 1739–57, Figuren von Ägidius Verhelst. Oben: *Füssen, Allgäu.* Ehemalige Klosterkirche St. Mang,
Engelreigen unter der Kanzel. Nach 1717, von Johann Anton Sturm.

Architecture, as if drawn into movement by sculpture. Left: Pilgrimage church *In der Wies near Steingaden, Upper Bavaria.*
View into the choir. 1739–57, figures by Ägidius Verhelst. Above: *Füssen, Allgäu.* Former convent church of St. Mang.
Putti, from the pulpit. Post 1717, by Johann Anton Sturm.

173

Foto Marburg

Links: Kirche *In der Wies*. Vom Gegenlicht
wie verklärt: der hl. Ambrosius. 1739–57,
von Johann Anton Sturm.

Left: Pilgrimage church *In der Wies*.
St. Ambrose. 1739–57,
by Johann Anton Sturm.

Rechts: *Berlin-Dahlem*. Staatl. Museen.
Weltlich kapriziös die Jungfrau Maria.
Fragment eines Altars. Holz. Alte Fassung.
Um 1760, von Joseph Anton Feuchtmayer.
(Vgl. farbiges Titelbild.)

Right: *Berlin-Dahlem*. Staatl. Museen. The Virgin
Mary. Dress and expression seem essentially
of this world. Fragment of an altar. C. 1760,
by Joseph Anton Feuchtmayer (q. v. col. frontis.).

   Foto Marburg

Birnau am Bodensee. Wallfahrtskirche. Ein Putto als „Honigschlecker". Vom Bernhardsaltar. Stuck. 1746–50, von J. A. Feuchtmayer.

Birnau, Lake Constance. Pilgrimage church. A putto as "honey thief." From the St. Bernard altar. Stucco. 1746–50, by J. A. Feuchtmayer.

Überlingen am Bodensee. Museum. Christophorus aus der Reichlin-Meldeggschen Hauskapelle. 1750, von J. A. Feuchtmayer.

Überlingen, Lake Constance. Museum. St. Christopher, from the private chapel of the Reichlin-Meldegg family. 1750, by J. A. Feuchtmayer.

Schmidt-Glassner

Volkstümliche Innigkeit, der Spätgotik verwandt, im Werk des Johann Joseph Christian. Links: *Ottobeuren, Schwaben*. Klosterkirche. Heiliger Dominikus vom Hauptaltar im West-Querarm. Um 1760. Oben: *Buchau am Federsee*. Ehemalige Damen-Stiftskirche. Beichtstuhl. Heiliger Nikolaus von der Flüe. Um 1775.

The work of Johann Joseph Christian displays a mood of unaffected, simple piety. Left: *Ottobeuren, Swabia*. Convent church. St. Dominic, from the principal altar in the west transept. C. 1760. Above: *Buchau/Federsee*. Church of the former Ladies' convent. St. Nicholas von der Flüe. From a confessional. C. 1775.

179

Le Brun

Keetman

Zwiefalten, Württemberg. Klosterkirche. Antlitz eines Engels an der Kanzel. Um 1760, von Johann Joseph Christian.

Zwiefalten, Württemberg. Convent church. Face of an angel, from the pulpit. C. 1760, by Johann Joseph Christian.

Diessen am Ammersee. Taufkapelle der Klosterkirche. Freischwebende Plastik: ein Engel. Um 1760. Zuschreibung ungewiß.

Diessen/Ammersee. Convent church. Baptismal chapel. Floating angel. C. 1760. Attribution uncertain.

180

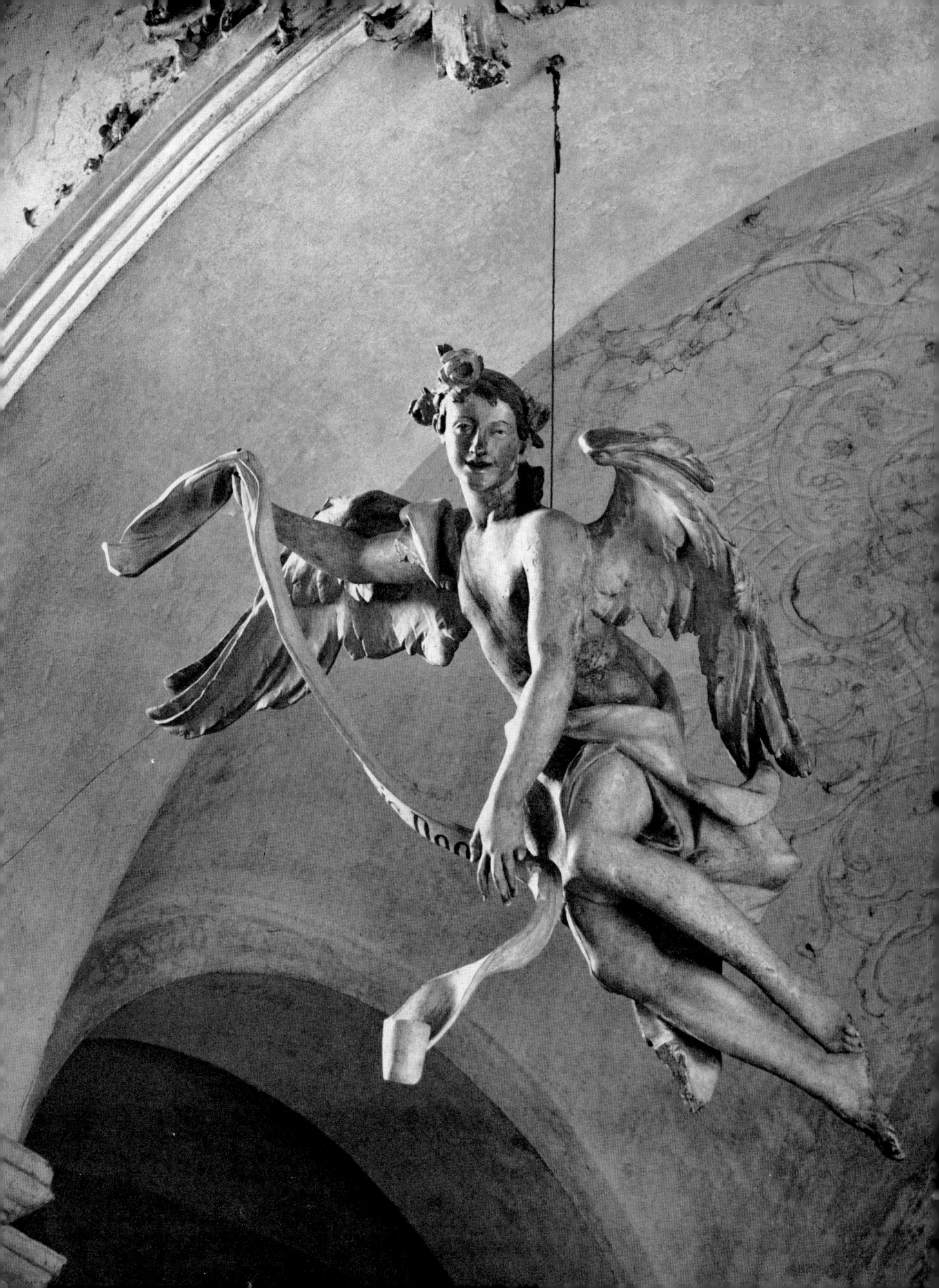

Birnau am Bodensee. Wallfahrtskirche. Putten am Hochaltar.
1746–50, von Joseph Anton Feuchtmayer.

Birnau, Lake Constance. Pilgrimage church. Putti on the High Altar.
1746–50, by Joseph Anton Feuchtmayer.

München. Bayerisches Nationalmuseum. Sizilianische Krippe. Terrakotta
und natürliche Werkstoffe. Spätes 18. Jh., von Giuseppe Sammartino.
Volkskunst erhebt sich zu künstlerischem Rang.

Munich. Bayerisches Nationalmuseum. Sicilian crib. Terracotta and natural
materials. Late 18th cent., by Giuseppe Sammartino.

Fiensch

Weyarn, Oberbayern. Klosterkirche. Rechts: Mariä Verkündigung. Holz. Alte Fassung. 1763, von Ignaz Günther. Oben: Ausschnitt. Weit ausfahrende Bewegungen kommen im Antlitz der Maria zur Ruhe.

Weyarn, Upper Bavaria. Convent church. Right: Annunciation. 1763, by Ignaz Günther. Above: detail. Agitated and expansive movements come to rest in the features of the Virgin.

Lockerung der Form durch ausgreifende Bewegung der Glieder in der letzten Phase des Barock. Oben: *Warkton Church, Northants*. Frauengruppe vom Grabmal der Herzogin von Montagu. Gestorben 1770. Von van Gelden. Rechts: *Rom*. St. Peter. Grabmal der Maria Clementina Sobieska. Gestorben 1735. Von Pietro Bracci.

A loosening of form through the expansive movement of the limbs in the last phase of the Baroque. Above: *Warkton Church, Northants* Mourning women, from the tomb of Mary, Duchess of   agu. D. 1770. By van Gelden. Right: *Rome*. St. Peter's. Tomb of Maria Clementina Sobieska. D. 1735. By Pietro Bracci.

Bauer

Pospesch

Prunk der Bibliotheken im Spätbarock. Oben: *Waldsassen, Bayer. Wald.* Bibliothek der ehemaligen Zisterzienserabtei. Der Bibliothekar.
1724–25, von Karl Stilp. Rechts: *Admont, Steiermark.* Bibliothek der Benediktinerabtei. Der Tod. Um 1760, von Taddäus Stammel.

The splendour of Late Baroque libraries. Above: *Waldsassen, Bavarian Forest.* The librarian. 1724–25, by Karl Stilp. Right: *Admont, Styria.*
Library of the Benedictine abbey. Death. C. 1760, by Taddäus Stammel.

Edwin Smith

Grcevic

Laibach, Jugoslawien. Flußgott am Brunnen der vier krainischen Flüsse.
1751, von Francesco Robba.

Ljubljana, Yugoslavia. River god, from the fountain of the four rivers
of Carniola. 1751, by Francesco Robba.

Queluz, Portugal. Putten im Schloßpark.
2. Hälfte 18. Jahrhundert.

Queluz, Portugal. Putti in the palace grounds.
2nd half 18th cent.

Vorliebe für exotische wie antike Motive. *Potsdam*. Park von Sanssouci. Oben: Trinkender Chinese am Teehaus. Sandstein, vergoldet. 1754–56, von Johann Peter Benkert. Rechts: Merkur. 1748, von Jean Baptiste Pigalle. (Original in den Staatlichen Museen, Berlin.)

Exotic as well as Classic motifs find favour. *Potsdam*. Park of Sanssouci. Above: a Chinese tea drinker, from the tea house. Gilt sandstone. 1754–56, by Johann Peter Benkert. Right: Mercury. 1748, by Jean Baptiste Pigalle. (Original in the Staatliche Museen, Berlin.)

Mit dem Beginn der Epoche des Barock gewinnt die Gebrauchskunst an Verbreitung und künstlerischem Rang. Oben: *Wien.*
Kunsthistorisches Museum. Salzfaß für König Franz I. von Frankreich. Gold. 1539–43, von Benvenuto Cellini. (Ausschnitt: Neptun.)

Since the beginning of the Baroque age, the decorative arts assume increasing importance. *Vienna.* Kunsthistorisches Museum.
Salt cellar for King Francis I of France. Gold. 1539–43, by Benvenuto Cellini (detail: Neptune).

Dresden. Grünes Gewölbe.
Tafelaufsatz. Das sogenannte
„Bad der Diana".
Chalzedonschale in goldener
Fassung mit Elfenbeinfiguren
und Email. Vor 1705,
von Johann Melchior Dinglinger.

Dresden. Grünes Gewölbe.
Centre piece. The so-called
"Bath of Diana." Chalcedony
bowl, mounted in gold with
ivory figures and enamel.
Pre 1705, by Johann Melchior
Dinglinger.

Rijksmuseum Amsterdam

Das Porzellan, für Europa neu
erfunden, wird zum bevorzugten
Werkstoff der Kleinkunst
des Rokoko.
Links: *Amsterdam*. Rijksmuseum.
Harlekin und Kolombine.
Meißener Porzellan. Nach 1740,
von Johann Joachim Kändler.
Rechts: *München*. Bayerisches
Nationalmuseum. Pantalone.
Nymphenburger Porzellan. 1755–63,
von Franz Anton Bustelli.

Porcelain, in Europe a new
invention, becomes a favourite
material of the Rococo sculptor.
Left: *Amsterdam*. Rijksmuseum.
Harlequin and Colombine. Meissen
porcelain. Post 1740, by Johann
Joachim Kändler.
Right: *Munich*. Bayerisches
Nationalmuseum. Pantalone.
Nymphenburg porcelain. 1755–63,
by Franz Anton Bustelli.

Links: *London*. Victoria and Albert Museum. Die Furcht. Buchsbaum. 3. Viertel 18. Jh., von einem süddeutschen Meister.

Left: *London*. Victoria and Albert Museum. Fear. Boxwood. 3rd quarter 18th cent., by a South German master.

Rechts: *Darmstadt*. Porzellanschlößchen. Der Winter. Kelsterbacher Porzellan. 1763, von Cornelius Carlstadt.

Right: *Darmstadt*. Porzellanschlösschen. Winter. Kelsterbach porcelain. 1763, by Cornelius Carlstadt.

Bauer

Gößweinstein, Oberfranken. Wallfahrtskirche. Hochaltar. Entwurf von J. M. Küchel, Bildhauerarbeiten von Johann Peter Benkert. 1740.
Links: Pyramidenhafter Aufbau, gipfelnd in dem spätgotischen Gnadenbild einer Marienkrönung. Oben: Kopf des Paulus.

Gössweinstein, Upper Franconia. Pilgrimage church. High Altar. Designed by J. M. Küchel, sculpture by Johann Peter Benkert. 1740.
Left: the pyramid-like composition, culminating in a Late Gothic mercy picture of the Coronation of the Virgin. Above: Head of St. Paul.

Seeger-Müller

Schneiders

Reichtum der Kirchenausstattung. Links: *Ottobeuren, Schwaben*. Klosterkirche. Chorgestühl mit Orgel. Um 1750–64, von J. J. Christian.
Oben: *St. Gallen, Schweiz*. Ehemalige Klosterkirche. Ein Relief vom Chorgestühl. 1768–69, von J. J. Christian oder J. A. Feuchtmayer.

The lavishness of Baroque church interior. Left: *Ottobeuren, Swabia*. Convent church. Choir stalls and organ. C. 1750–64, by Johann Joseph Christian.
Above: *St. Gall, Switzerland*. Former convent church. Relief from the choir stalls. 1768–69, by J. J. Christian or J. A. Feuchtmayer.

203

Bauer

Links: *Vierzehnheiligen,
Oberfranken*. Wallfahrtskirche.
Der Gnadenaltar der Vierzehn
Nothelfer. 1763. Entwurf von
J. M. Küchel, ausgeführt von
J. M. Feichtmayr und
J. G. Übelherr.

Left: *Vierzehnheiligen, Upper
Franconia*. Pilgrimage church.
The mercy altar of the
Fourteen Helpers in Need. 1763.
Designed by J. M. Küchel,
executed by J. M. Feichtmayr
and J. G. Übelherr.

Rechts: *Hamburg*. Museum für
Kunst und Gewerbe. Neptun und
Amphitrite. Entwurf einer
Brunnengruppe für Schloß
Seehof bei Bamberg. Um 1748,
von Johann Ferdinand Dietz.

Right: *Hamburg*. Museum für
Kunst und Gewerbe. Neptune
and Amphitrite. Model of a
fountain group for Schloss
Seehof near Bamberg.
C. 1748, by Johann
Ferdinand Dietz.

Museum für Kunst
und Gewerbe Hamburg

Busch

Links: *Würzburg.* Schloß.
Nischenfiguren im Kaisersaal.
1749—51, von Antonio Bossi.

Left: *Würzburg.* Palace. Figures
in the Kaisersaal. 1749—51,
by Antonio Bossi.

Rechts: *Würzburg.* Museum auf
der Veste Marienberg. Merkur,
aus dem Park des Schlosses
Veitshöchheim. Nach 1763,
von Johann Ferdinand Dietz.

Right: *Würzburg.* Museum on
the Veste Marienberg. Mercury,
from the park of Schloss
Veitshöchheim. Post 1763,
by Johann Ferdinand Dietz.

London. Royal Academy of Arts. Stürzender Titan. 1786, von Thomas Banks.

London. Royal Academy. Falling Titan. 1786, by Thomas Banks.

Paris. Louvre. Prometheus. 1762, von Nicolas Sebastian Adam.

Paris. Louvre. Prometheus. 1762, by Nicolas Sebastian Adam.

Ende der Epoche: Die barocken Grabmäler werden naturalistisch sentimental. Oben: *Paris*. Notre-Dame. Grabmal für Henry Claude d'Harcourt. 1774, von Jean Baptiste Pigalle. Rechts: *London*. Westminster Abbey. Nightingale-Grabmal. 1761, von Louis François Roubiliac.

The end of an epoch: Baroque tombs become naturalistic and sentimental. Above: *Paris*. Notre-Dame. Tomb of Henry Claude d'Harcourt. 1774, by Jean Baptiste Pigalle. Right: *London*. Westminster Abbey. Nightingale tomb. 1761, by Louis François Roubiliac.

21

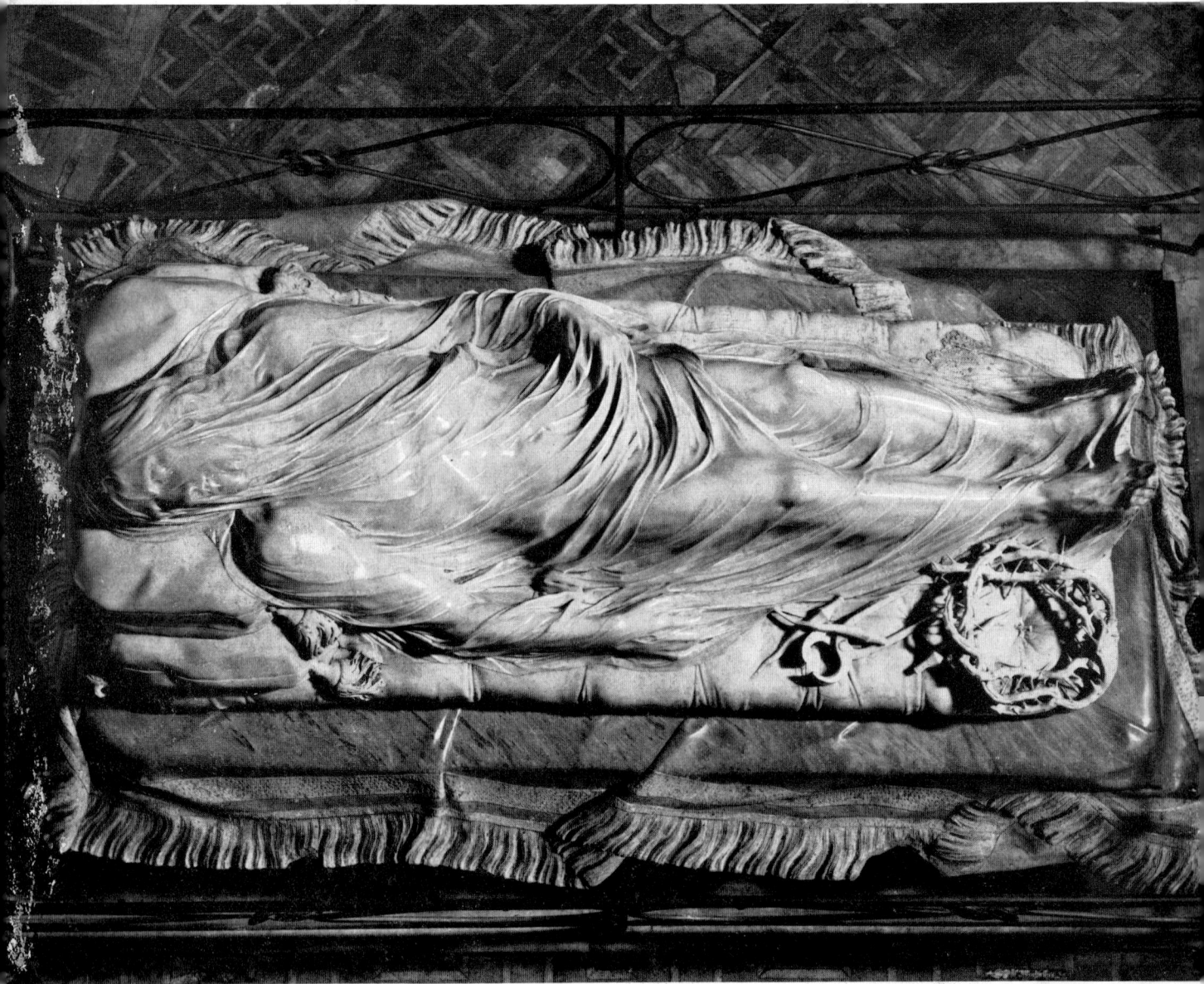

Der Gedanke an den Tod — immer gegenwärtig in einem Zeitalter frühen Sterbens. Oben: *Neapel*. Cappella Sansevero. Leichnam Christi,
in ein Leichentuch eingehüllt. 1752, von Giuseppe Sammartino. Rechts: *Salem nahe dem Bodensee*. Ehemalige Klosterkirche. Der Tod und der Abt.
Alabaster. Um 1774—94, von einem der Nachfolger Feuchtmayers, entweder Georg Dirr oder J. G. Wieland.

The thought of death, ever-present in an age when men were short-lived. Above: *Naples*. Cappella Sansevero. Dead Christ, wrapped in a shroud.
1752, by Giuseppe Sammartino. Right: *Salem, near Lake Constance*. Former convent church. Death and the abbot. Alabaster.
C. 1774—94, by one of Feuchtmayer's successors, either Georg Dirr or J. G. Wieland.

212

In Spanien ist das Ende des Barock gekennzeichnet durch Übersteigerung des Naturalismus. *Murcia*. Museo Salzillo (Ermita de Jesús). Antlitz Christi von einer Kreuztragungsgruppe (mit echtem Menschenhaar). Um 1780, von Francisco Antonio Salzillo.

In Spain, the end of the Baroque is marked by an accentuated realism. *Murcia*. Museo Salzillo (Ermita de Jesús). Real human hair has been used. Christ carrying His cross. C. 1780, by Francisco Antonio Salzillo.

Murcia, Spanien. Ermita de Jesús. Abendmahl (der Tisch mit echtem Leinentuch). Um 1780, von Francisco Antonio Salzillo.

Murcia, Spain. Ermita de Jesús. Last Supper. The table is laid with a real tablecloth. C. 1780, by Francisco Antonio Salzillo.

Zum Bild der folgenden Seite: *London.* Victoria and Albert Museum. Schwebender Engel. Mitte 18. Jh., von einem unbekannten süddeutschen Meister.

On the following page: *London.* Victoria and Albert Museum. Floating angel. Mid 18th cent., by an unknown South German master.